The story of

The Eagles

The Long Run　　**Marc Shapiro**

The story of

The Eagles

The Long Run   **Marc Shapiro**

OMNIBUS PRESS

London / New York / Paris

Copyright © 1995 Omnibus Press
(A Division of Book Sales Limited)

Edited by Chris Charlesworth.
Picture research by Nikki Russell.

ISBN 0-7119-4817-8
Order No. OP 47550

Exclusive Distributors:
Book Sales Limited
8/9 Frith Street,
London W1V 5TZ, UK.

Music Sales Corporation
257 Park Avenue South,
New York, NY 10010, USA.

Music Sales Pty Limited
120 Rothschild Avenue, Rosebery,
NSW 2018, Australia.

To the Music Trade only:
Music Sales Limited
8/9 Frith Street,
London W1V 5TZ, UK.

Front Cover inset picture from Pictorial Press.

Every effort has been made to trace
the copyright holders of the photographs
in this book but one or two were
unreachable. We would be grateful if
the photographers concerned would
contact us.

Printed in the United Kingdom by
Redwood Books Limited, Trowbridge, Wiltshire.

A catalogue record for this book is
available from the British Library.

Contents

Most authors write their introductions before getting down to the meat and potatoes of their subject. But I'm going to be honest with you. When I sat down to chronicle the history of The Eagles, the meat and potatoes came first. Why? Because I was not quite sure how to set the table.

Oh, I was definitely a fan. You couldn't turn on your car radio while bopping down the road in the Seventies and not be instantly drawn into the simple, idyllic but always thoughtful strains of 'Take It Easy' or 'Peaceful Easy Feeling'. Even when they grew up, got serious and hit us with 'Hotel California', 'Life In The Fast Lane' and 'One Of These Nights', the buzz was still there. Love them or hate them (and, to be sure, most critics dismissed them as a plague), The Eagles knew their way around a song. They had 16 of those puppies in the Top 40, five of them reaching number one and eight (nine if you count their comeback disc 'Hell Freezes Over') albums that sold in the millions.

That in itself, while no mean feat, is a fairly common occurrence. What is uncommon is the intangibles that made this group of Californian musicians, by way of all over the map, stand head and shoulders above the big hair bands and poseurs that populated the music world when The Eagles first landed. And as I did my research, talked to those who would talk and attempted to get into the personalities of the band members, one constant kept popping out. And that was a real sense of destiny.

The Eagles were going to happen whether we wanted them to or not. It was on the cards. It was a plan. It was a vision born of individual, uncompromising creative desires that found their way to Southern California where fate, luck, talent and an overriding sense of purpose came together.

The Eagles were not your typical rock and roll alliance. To be sure they were human. They were out for the usual perks; the women, the money, the hits and the best kind of ego boost of all, respect. Like most bands who wear their hearts on their sleeves, they regularly fell prey to a myriad of vices. Drugs were a regular fly in the ointment. Booze was never far behind.

But what enabled The Eagles to consistently rise from the wreckage and fly again was a maddeningly dedicated approach to making memorable music and writing classic songs. They were not the typical pop fodder to be ground up and spat out in the name of corporate bottom lines. What they were and continue to be are primitives, purists and virgins in long hair and jeans if you will who, from the word go, intent on creating their own musical universe without so much as a second glance at whatever obstacles that stood in their way.

The successes mounted up. But with them came that old demon integrity that, throughout the life of the band, was a constant source of bedevilment. It was a trait that secured their place in history but it was a tough cross to bear. It was a constant source of hard feelings and studio and road battles.

Whatever the circumstances, you don't bail on a band that's accumulating riches as big as the National Debt because you can't stomach the colour of money and the smell of success. But that's exactly what Bernie Leadon and Randy Meisner did. You don't start out friends and end up hating the sight of each other. But that was the Odyssey ultimately travelled by Glenn Frey and Don Henley. And, perhaps more telling, you don't just decide to pack it in when the creative curve, despite what many people feel about 'The Long Run', is still climbing. But, in 1982, that's exactly what The Eagles did.

The Eagles were a tough act to walk away from but, as most members have readily admitted over the years, the very drive that was keeping them together, to create as perfect a musical world as possible, was also slowly but surely tearing them apart. It was painful. It was bloody. It hurt like hell. But in their minds it was simply time to call it quits.

It was a division that ran so deep that, during the ensuing years, Frey and Henley regularly balked at big money offers to reunite and let The Eagles fly again. They didn't really need the money. And they certainly didn't need the pressure of having to deal with each other once again.

For The Eagles to regroup it had to be right in a way that most people can't begin to understand. And finally it was.

When they did decide to reunite in 1994, it did not seem like The Eagles had been apart for 14 years. Lyrically and musically they sounded as inspiring as ever. Live, their tour was that rarity, an *event*. This was the show you had to be at for all the right reasons.

How long the reunited Eagles will continue to fly is anybody's guess. Even before the 'Hell Freezes Over' tour had reached its mid-point, there were already rumblings from different members that some of the old problems, the ego trips that tore them apart before, were still there. But, however long The Eagles decide to ride the wave, it's been good to have them back in our lives. And finally it is the drive to create that makes The Eagles real, and any book that attempts to make sense of their rise and fall worthwhile.

For The Eagles are an ornate, occasionally roughly fractured mirror. A mirror that reflects on the possibilities of music as something very personal and permanent in our lives and in what goes into painting that picture. The Eagles were the master plan. They're what destiny is all about.

Marc Shapiro, March 1995

I would like to thank former Eagle Randy Meisner for giving me a bird's eye view of the band in motion. Thanks also to former Eagle Bernie Leadon who, despite refusing to be interviewed for this book, was cordial and encouraging by telephone and fax. Several attempts to contact and interview the current line-up of The Eagles were unsuccessful.

I would like to thank the following credited publications, books and television documentaries for their wealth of resource material *Rolling Stone*, *The Los Angeles Times*, *Time Magazine*, *Goldmine*, *Musician*, *Melody Maker*, *GQ*, *Billboard*, *Crawdaddy*, *The Record Producers*, *The Way I See It*, *Off The Record* and *Eagles: A Family Tree* and the cast of characters at Poo Bah Records.

Finally thanks to Chris Charlesworth at Omnibus Press for giving me this shot.

To my wife, Nancy, and daughter, Rachael, who put up with the madness during the writing of this book. This Eagle's for you. To Bennie and Freda who have the best seats in rock and roll heaven.

Chapter I

Hell Freezes Over

Long Beach, California. 1980. Summer slowly bleeding into Fall.

On the floor of the cavernous Long Beach Arena, a well heeled group of hip young Democrats are whooping it up for their candidate of the moment, Senator Alan Cranston, and the band who've come to perform tonight on his financial behalf, The Eagles.

Backstage the fuse that would blow The Eagles off the map is about to be lit.

"What did you say?" yelled Glenn Frey, turning to confront Don Felder. Frey felt Henley had insulted Senator Cranston under his breath, and needed to confront him with it.

Before the scene could turn uglier than it already was, cooler heads separated the pair. Moments later the Master of Ceremonies out front introduced the band. Amid thunderous applause, Frey, Felder, Don Henley, Timothy B. Schmit and Joe Walsh took the stage, flashing forced smiles to mask the tension that gripped the band.

The Eagles launched into a set of familiar greatest hits. Music that had defined and shaped the attitudes of the Seventies echoed throughout the arena. The Democrats loved it. But up on stage the battle lines were being drawn as the set wound down.

"We were on stage," remembered Frey, "and Felder looks back at me and says 'Only three more songs until I kick your ass pal.' And I'm saying 'Great! I can't wait.' We were out there singing 'Best Of My Love' but inside both of us were thinking 'As soon as this is over, I'm gonna kill him...'"

The Eagles finished their set, acknowledged their applause with as much good grace as they could muster and stormed back to the dressing room. No sooner had the door closed behind them than Frey was in Felder's face, screaming. Felder screamed back, grabbed his guitar by the neck and slammed it against a wall, reducing it to splinters. Less than an hour earlier, up on stage, they'd been singing 'Take It Easy' and 'Peaceful Easy Feeling'.

"For me it ended in Long Beach, California," said Frey later. "That was when I knew I had to get out."

The official end to the band was still a few months off. Obliged to mix the tapes for an upcoming live album, four of them flew to Miami to complete the work. Frey refused to join the others, so the tapes were flown back and forth between Miami and Frey's home in Los Angeles in order that the record could be completed in time for its projected Christmas 1980 release. The unofficial break-up had become so complete in the band members' minds that not even the offer of an additional $2 million advance from Asylum Records for just two new songs on the live album could get The Eagles to fly one more time.

Don Henley received a long distance telephone call from Frey later that year that, to his way of thinking, made the split final.

"Glenn called me up one day and told me he wanted to go and do some recording on his own," Henley told GQ in 1991. "It was a casual conversation that started out being about football, and then he interjected that he wanted to go do something on his own. He didn't necessarily mean by that that he wanted to break up the group but it pissed me off so bad because I always thought in my mind that, when the group broke up, we'd get in a room together and get good and drunk and sort of cry on each others' shoulders and say 'Well it was great and I love you and we're just gonna quit now. I don't think he meant it to be that abrupt but it was just too painful for him to do it any other way.

"It scared me also as a matter of fact. For a few months I was pacing in the house and drinking a lot. That was really a rough time for me."

The Eagles continued in name only until May 1982 when the official split was announced by manager Irving Azoff. Azoff, who claimed that "Frey and Henley realised they didn't need the group any more and that they could make great solo records" always felt an Eagles' break-up was imminent.

"The Eagles were breaking up from the day I met them," he said. "At the end of every tour they broke up. There is no date as to an actual break-up. One day they just kind of drifted into a divorce."

Don Felder put it more succinctly.

"When it stops being fun, it's time to do something else. It's time to check out."

But for Frey a sense of bitterness seemed to linger when he proclaimed in a 1982 conversation: "There'll never be a 'Greed and Lost Youth' tour."

The reluctance would continue for Frey as the years rolled by. Unlike Don Henley's, his solo career never really took off, but the offers to return The Eagles to the flight path continued to roll in. As recently as 1992, his mind remained unchanged. "There is not going to be an Eagles' reunion," he said. "I'd see it as a step backward. Nothing about it appeals to me."

December 6, 1993. A rehearsal room in Los Angeles.

Glenn Frey, Don Henley, Don Felder, Joe Walsh and Timothy B. Schmit are tuning up. Rehearsals for the 'Greed and Lost Youth' tour? Not yet. The former Eagles have agreed to regroup for a video behind country star Travis Tritt, covering The Eagles' classic song 'Take It Easy'. The video will be used to goose sales of an Irving Azoff driven tribute album 'Common Thread: The Songs Of The Eagles', versions of Eagles' songs by top country music stars.

"I said the only way I'd do the video is if they could get The Eagles back together," recalled Tritt. "Everybody laughed because nobody thought it would happen. But when Giant (Azoff's fledgling record label) approached them and they agreed, I was scared to death because I was expecting a fist fight."

The one day taping goes smoothly. The expected tension failed to materialise. Frey and Walsh, Henley, Felder and Schmit, and, most importantly, Frey and Henley, seemed to be getting along. But, at the end of the day, nobody was willing to concede much more than a congenial day.

"The Tritt video was fun," offered Schmit. "But that's as far as it went. I am not going to start thinking 'What if?'. I am just going ahead with my plans for the summer."

Henley, for his part, would only agree that... "I think we have a heightened appreciation of what kind of legacy we created."

But, as the band members were preparing to leave, Henley and Frey walked over to each other, hugged and said "Let's get together real soon and talk."

The Eagles returned to their different worlds. Henley's ongoing passion was now conservation, specifically the saving of Walden Woods, the 2,680 acres of largely unspoiled New England forest in Concord, Massachusetts, where poet/writer Henry David Thoreau wrote his classic work *Walden*. Henley became involved in this project because Thoreau's work made a deep impression on him while he was growing up in Texas.

For Frey it was the easy life with his wife Cindy, a choreographer, their two children, and dividing his time between the recording studio and the golf course. Walsh was surviving the trauma of his recent divorce by working out on soundtracks and session work. Felder, who had become frustrated with music and had embarked on a successful career in real estate, was content to live the peaceful easy life with his wife Susan and their four children. Schmit was preparing for yet another assault on a largely dormant solo career, and playing homebody with his wife Jean and their two children.

April 1994. A sound stage in Burbank ,California.

"Stop!" yells Glenn Frey from a stage where The Eagles have been running through a set that includes such familiar tunes as 'Life In The Fast Lane', 'One Of These Nights' and the newly penned songs, 'The Girl From Yesterday' and 'Get Over It'. "I'm having trouble hearing the piano in the sound mix. I'm hearing a lot of drop-off."

15

Frey walks to the centre, cosies up to the engineer and listens as the engineer turns some knobs and the overall sound comes into synch. Satisfied, Frey returns to the stage. He walks over to Walsh and Felder, compliments them with a "nice guitar parts" and returns to the stage where the band continues to rehearse for a comeback that has been 14 years in the making.

"It was frustrating at first," said Walsh during a break in their pre-flight rehearsals for The Eagles' second coming. "We were rusty at first. We really wanted to do it. We wanted to get our chops back to show people that we were not has-beens and that we could still rock. As things progressed with the rehearsals and stuff I knew we still had it, but playing on a rehearsal stage to a bunch of roadies and sound people is a whole lot different than playing in front of an audience. But once we got into it, it didn't sound like we had been apart 14 years. It only sounded like we had taken a week off."

Joe Smith, former chairman of Elektra Entertainment, where the first wave of Eagles' recordings emerged, was not surprised by the reunion; only that it took this long.

"This could have happened five years ago," he offered early in 1994. "They were best friends for years. They lived together and shared everything together. I'm sure they finally figured what's the use of wasting time and energy being at war."

Felder, picking tunefully during a break, agreed.

"When we got back together we realised that we had enough time to just bury a lot of those old feelings. Everybody had just gotten over it. But one of the questions that just kept piercing our minds was can we do this again? Can we be as good as we were? Because nobody wanted to go out there and be less than our expectations and we sure didn't want to come across as less than what the public thought of us."

"We've all grown up a lot," said Frey when the rehearsal ended for the day. "I don't live in the past. As far as I'm concerned this is Day One."

Henley, leaving for the day, agreed. "Getting back together is normal. The abnormal thing was breaking up in the first place. I guess you could say that our new song 'Get Over It' has become our new theme song. That song and maybe 'The Heart Of The Matter' which is about forgiving and forgetting."

The song 'Get Over It' was also of particular importance to Frey. "Don and I were sitting there writing this song and we found ourselves getting really excited about it. It was a great feeling to know that, after 14 years, we could still get together and make the magic happen."

It is another day on the rehearsal stage. The string section of a local orchestra is running through an intro to one of The Eagles' songs. The members of the band are lounging on chairs and amps, listening intently. The strings start into their part.

"Stop," said Henley as he walked over to confer with the conductor and check the music. "There's a bit of harmony that's not quite right. I can tell."

He walked to the other side of the stage and groused under his breath. "They're playing like white people. Blues man! Let's try the blues!"

It is a month later. April 1994. A line of lucky audience members snakes outside a Burbank studio. They've come a long way to hear The Eagles' official return in the form of an MTV concert that is being taped for an airing later in the year. Inside video and audio machinery is being adjusted by technicians. Cameras are being positioned through the rows of chairs for the best possible coverage. Roadies wander on and off the stage checking mikes and strumming guitars for the best possible sound. The hustle and bustle is not lost on Felder who is sitting nearby, watching the action.

"There's a lot of pressure," he conceded. "It's not like we're just going in and playing a bar gig. We've really stepped back into The Eagles pressure cooker."

Walsh and Frey confer briefly in an audience area that will be filled to capacity in a couple of hours. Frey mentions to Walsh that it would be a good idea if everybody but the band were out of the backstage area 30 minutes before the show starts. He claps Walsh on the back. They are laughing, smiling. It was a moment that was not lost on Felder after the show.

"Everybody was feeling pretty good before we went out. It was interesting to see how well everybody was handling it. What a difference the few years of maturing has made. There was a kind of warmth that relieved the pressure and stress. That warmth had not been there a lot of times in the past."

It is mere minutes before The Eagles go on stage again for the first time in 14 years. Backstage, amid a jumble of equipment trucks and band trailers, there is a mixture of excitement and nerves. Schmit appears the most animated, wandering the makeshift compound, chattering nervously with a perpetual smile on his face. Walsh is wandering in and out of his trailer, a firm grip on his guitar slung low in his hand. Henley is in his trailer. He does not want to be disturbed.

"Nervous?" said Schmit. "Yeah I'm a little nervous."

"For us to make the MTV shows our first live gigs and knowing they would be broadcast was pretty ballsy and pretty stupid on our part," Schmit would say later. "But it was almost like the way it had to be. It was like 'Here we go! Let's do it!'"

Felder, after the show, painted a vivid picture of what was going on in the heads of The Eagles moments before they hit the stage. "You know what it's like when you've had too many cups of coffee? Well that's the kind of nervous and unsettled we were. We knew we had rehearsed really well. We knew the songs. But the first time we walked back on the stage as a band and played in public it was like putting the key back in the ignition and turning it over for the first time. Well you know how that can get."

The band has gathered in the wings. The audience's whoops and hollers have reached a crescendo. The applause is deafening. Last minute jitters are played down with a particular piece of psycho drama when Felder turned to Frey and, in good natured homage to the incident that finally brought the band down, said, "I'm going to kick your ass!"

Everybody bursts out laughing. Frey, in response, turned light-heartedly serious.

"Gentlemen," he intoned, "it's good to be with you. I hope I'm with you always."

During the performance, Henley took a moment in his introduction to the song 'New York Minute', to tell the audience exactly what it meant to be back. "This song is about appreciating what you have. We're all very happy to be friends again. We're happy our music has survived and that we have survived because, in this industry, that's not easy."

The Eagles were back and in a very big way. The band's MTV concert aired in October 1994. A live album of that taping, entitled 'Hell Freezes Over', which also included four new Eagles' compositions, 'Get Over It', 'Love Will Keep Us Alive', 'Learn To Be Still' and 'The Girl From Yesterday', was released the following month and immediately shot to the top of the charts. It proved to be the perfect stop-gap album in that it answered all the important questions: yes, the band could still play; yes, Frey and Henley could still write decent songs; and, yes, they seemed to be having fun. But the most anticipated wing of this Eagles' reflight was the band's first live shows since the 1980 blow-up in Long Beach, that kicked off in late May of 1994 and continued on well into 1995.

The cash generated by their decision to fly again was staggering. Projected tour revenues, with tickets priced at a hefty $115, were estimated at $150 million, while record sales were also expected to reach into the $150 million range.

The shows were designed to showcase The Eagles' legacy to maximum effect. Each one opened with the haunting introduction to 'Hotel California', as instantly recognisable as any piece of music in the band's entire catalogue, and thereafter the group treated their audience to a mixture of new material, including 'Get Over It', 'The Girl From Yesterday' and 'Love Will Keep Us Alive', and familiar chestnuts, from oldies like 'Take It Easy' and 'Tequila Sunrise' to more up-tempo material like 'Life In The Fast Lane'. The two hour set climaxed with a rousing, heartfelt rendition of 'Desperado'.

But Henley, shortly before the tour began, was already thinking in terms of this second Eagles' grouping as more than a one shot money maker. "The truth is, they have been offering us buckets of money every year to get us back together, but there is not enough money in the universe to get us to do this if we didn't want to do it.

"This feels more like a resumption to me," he continued. "There's no reason why, at this juncture, we can't have The Eagles and our solo careers too. We could have done that in the first place if we hadn't been so overwrought about everything."

The 'Hell Freezes Over' tour went off like clockwork. A total of 44 out of the first 45, primarily stadium and larger arena venues, sold out to the tune of 1.2 million fans. But the tour came to an abrupt halt on October 4, 1994, when Frey developed a stomach problem that required immediate surgery.

"Frey has a chronic gastro-intestinal problem and his doctor has told him it would be best if he postponed the rest of the tour," said Eagles' publicist Lisa Vega, reading from a prepared statement on October 3. Concert dates were rescheduled. Frey recovered from surgery and the band resumed touring in January of 1995.

The Eagles remain optimistic about a future together. And one of the most optimistic, post-surgery, is Frey. "Maybe we'll try and keep The Eagles together a little longer than we anticipated. I thought the four studio tracks we did on 'Hell Freezes Over' turned out really good and I think it would be great to do an entire studio album. There's that possibility and I'd certainly like to talk to the guys about it."

But Frey said it was an optimism mixed with equal parts caution. "This is something people have been wanting us to do for 14 years. So we've finally gone ahead and done it. I think we'll go on for a while and then take a break. At some point, I think we'll talk about doing it again.

"We all remember what happened last time and we remember the good and the bad. And we hope that we are all older and more mature now and can learn from the mistakes. So far it has been great.

But I think we are prepared, if it stops being fun, it will stop. Just as it stopped before."

The fun apparently stopped for Henley real quick. During a November 1994 interview, during the band's touring hiatus, Henley indicated that the resurrection of The Eagles would likely be a short one.

"I think after this tour, that will be it. Some of the things that broke us apart years ago have not gone away. I thought maybe they had. We've grown in different ways now, as people should and so we'll finish our obligations and go our separate ways again. And frankly I'm looking forward to that."

Those comments set off an immediate firestorm which to speculation, contrary to constant band denials, that The Eagles had only gotten back together for the bucks.

Henley stepped back from his remarks. His reason for the statements? "I was just having a bad day."

Chapter II

The Flight To The Promised Land

Although The Eagles and the music they made became synonymous with California and its laid back ambience, none of its fledgling members was born in America's Golden State.

Glenn Frey, who by dint of his standing in the middle on stage seemed somehow to be the band's leader and spokesman, was born in Detroit, Michigan, on November 6, 1948, which made him the youngest member of the original quartet. Although less than 2,000 miles away from the temperate Los Angeles terrain that Frey would celebrate in song, spiritually Detroit might as well be on the other side of the globe. The centre of America's car industry, it is an unlovely urban sprawl without a palm tree in sight and where, in winter, when the winds from Canada whip off Lake Erie and Lake St Clair, the temperature regularly dips to levels unheard of in the American South West.

Nevertheless Frey was a budding case of cool at an early age, mixing a high IQ with a growing sense of rugged individualism. Although undersized by most athletic standards, he was a triple threat jock through junior high school, excelling in Little League baseball, American football and wrestling in the hundred pound and below weight division.

And, according to those who grew up with him, Frey was also big on running his mouth. "He knew he was cool," recalled a girl who grew up within the Frey sphere of influence. "He was really into being this kind of teen king."

Frey's introduction to music began at age five when his parents made him take piano lessons which lasted until he was 12. "It wasn't very glamorous." He winced at the memory. "The kids who knew I was taking them could be pretty mean."

Frey's high school years, in a progressive oriented curriculum, helped shape his creative side. Reading, on a wide variety of topics, included the works of beat prince Jack Kerouac, and an early infatuation with the imagery of James Dean. A budding interest in writing was welling up inside and nobody, especially his teachers, with whom he was constantly at war, could tell him different.

"I once told Glenn that he reminded me of a rattlesnake," says his mother Nellie. "A rattlesnake coiled up in a corner ready to strike. If you pass by, you'd better listen for that rattle. Glenn loves that description. He has the courage to care through his beliefs. It may be ruthless but, to his way of thinking, you can't be a nice guy."

So it came as no surprise that Frey, during his high school years, discovered and took solace in rock and roll. The radio was always on when Glenn was around. He was even in the audience at Detroit's Olympia Hall where, on September 6, 1964, he saw two performances by The Beatles, both lasting around 30 minutes each.

"My aunt got tickets to see The Beatles and it was just an amazing experience," he recalled not too long ago. "You barely heard the beginnings of each song and then it was just these waves of people screaming. This girl in the chair in front of me fell into my arms. She was screaming 'Paul! Paul!' I thought 'Wow! Man! This is really cool!'"

In later life he would remember the impact those shows had on his career choice. "I had this dream about holding the spotlight as a rock star. That's when I decided to take up the guitar."

Frey learned to play guitar and during his teenage years worked an apprenticeship in various local Detroit bands, among them The Mushrooms, The Subterraneans and The Four Of Us. He had found his place on the stage and, in consideration of his libido, in the hearts of countless rock and roll groupies. To say that Frey was arrogant when it came to the opposite sex was an understatement.

"He took my sister out once," said a former Detroit neighbour, "and tried to feel her up. She didn't let him, so he brought her home early and never called her again."

Frey's mother Nellie was more diplomatic when discussing her guitar crazy-girl crazy son. "I remember telling him once that his life revolved around groups of people but that he couldn't relate well to individuals. I told him 'Glenn, if your guitar had tits and an ass, you'd never date another girl'."

Frey graduated from high school in 1966 and mother and son quickly butted heads. Nellie wanted Glenn to go to college. Frey wanted to stay in Detroit and continue to rock and roll. Nellie won the day by subterfuge. "I went to Bob Seger's manager (who was also the big thing booking wise in the Detroit area) and asked him to not give Glenn any bookings unless he stopped smoking marijuana and got good grades in college."

Frey took the hint, reluctantly went off to college but immediately began to make the most of the Seger connection. "Seger was cool. I was never in his band but he liked me and let me come to some sessions when he was recording. He let me play maracas and, on one song, he let me play acoustic guitar. I also got to sing backup vocals on Seger's song 'Ramblin' Gamblin' Man' which was like his first big hit."

But Frey was not content to be a relatively big fish in a fair to middling rock and roll town and, in 1968, after a stint backing Bo Diddley, he packed his bags and headed for Los Angeles. Music, he admitted later, was not the main reason for going West. "I was going to buy drugs in Mexico and see a girlfriend who had moved out there with her sister. My parents told me that if I was going to go to California, they weren't going to give me a goddamned dime."

But Nellie Frey said that she ultimately caved in. "Every time I would send him a letter I would put five or ten bucks in it. I would tell him 'buy yourself a nice breakfast and a pack of cigarettes'."

A tornado slammed through the town of Gilmer, Texas, on July 22, 1947, ripping up trees and mangling buildings. At its height, when the winds were blowing their fiercest, Don Henley came into the world.

The Henleys didn't stick around to survey the damage. His father, an auto parts store owner named CJ, and mother, an occasional school teacher named Hughlene, were so spooked by the tornado that they packed up the baby with their modest belongings and moved to an even smaller town called Linden, also in North East Texas, close to its borders with Arkansas and Louisiana.

But the intensity of the weather made its mark on the young Henley's psyche, according to childhood friend and one-time bandmate Richard Bowden. "Don's always been tense," he said in 1979. "When he solves one problem, he just moves on to something else to worry about."

Henley's wonder years in Linden consisted of dabbling in football, fighting a losing battle with the trombone and dealing with the inevitable small town boredom. "In a town like that, all you can do is dream," he would say years later. "There wasn't anything you could do but sit and watch the sun sink in the west."

Linden was not unlike the kind of town that Peter Bogdonavich depicted in his famous black and white movie *The Last Picture Show*. It was not a town that coveted intelligence but, according to his high school English teacher Margaret Lovelace, speaking in a 1991 *GQ* interview, intelligence was something Don Henley never lacked. "He always had something to say about almost every subject. He was a good writer and he had a good command of the language."

Henley was also quite good at playing the good old boy game. "I made good grades but I also got drunk and threw up every day," he admits.

When Henley discovered music he also discovered the drums, but his ragged relationship with his father, and the general lack of disposable funds in the family, meant that a major extravagance such as a drum kit was unlikely. So Henley and his more sympathetic mother cooked up a scheme together. First he blew up the family's antiquated laundry cauldron with a cherry bomb, thus forcing the acquisition of a more modern washing machine for his mum. In return, she agreed to go around her husband and grant Henley his first set of $600 drums.

His mother remembered: "We didn't know how his father would react. So we didn't tell him what we were doing. Don and I drove fifty miles to the music store to buy them and then we took them to his father's store. He was a bit stunned but he agreed to go along with it."

Henley reached a turning point in 1962 when he accepted an offer to put his primitive drum skills to work in a local Dixieland jazz band. Rock came into the picture during the summer of 1963 with Henley playing the drums in the local band, The Four Speeds, which included his friend Richard Bowden, his brother Mike and later Eagles producer/string arranger Jim Ed Norman on keyboards. Like so many others of the time, the band specialised in instrumentals. "But we eventually realised that vocals were where it's at," recalled Bowden, "but nobody wanted to sing. So we put our names in a bowl and drew one out. Don lost and became our singer."

The Four Speeds changed their name to The Speed and then, as Felicity, released one single on a local label called 'Hurtin''. "We went through a number of small time managers and played a lot of frat houses," remembered Henley.

Rock gave way to bluegrass in 1965 when, while at a Shreveport, Louisiana concert ostensibly to see The Byrds, he discovered the opening act, The Dillards. "I was shocked," related Henley during an early Seventies interview. "They really knocked me off my seat. I had never heard anything like it before."

In short order Felicity became Shiloh, a frat house favourite capable of pulling down $500 a night and testing the cultural waters in a largely redneck region. "We were hair pioneers," recalled Henley with a laugh in 1991. "I was the first guy in town to smoke grass and to have my hair touch my ears."

Henley continued to immerse himself in the music while continuing at college, at Stephen Austin State University and North Texas State, but this was more out of habit than with any specific academic goal in mind. After four years he left college with no degree but the sound advice of an out-of-step English teacher was ringing in his ears. "One day he told me, 'Your parents are asking me what your future plans are. I know there's a lot of pressure on you to decide.' Then he said 'If it takes you your whole fucking life to find out what you want to do, you should take it'. I never forgot that."

A chance meeting with Kenny Rogers, then fronting The First Edition, inspired Shiloh to drop its copy band status in favour of original material and to make plans to move to Los Angeles. It was Henley's childhood fantasy come true. "I used to sit and watch the sun sink in the west and would say 'Boy, the sun's going down in California. Some day I'm going to be there.'

"California was the dream of success... the imagery, the music of The Beach Boys and The Byrds. It was the magazines I would read and the stuff I saw on television. Man... for me California was always the promised land."

Bernie Leadon was born in Minneapolis, Minnesota, on July 19, 1947, but his journey West was motivated not by his own ambitions but by those of his family. He was the only original Eagle to have a taste of actually growing up in California. The Leadon family moved to San Diego when Bernie was seven and it was here that he took an interest in folk music, becoming proficient at the guitar and banjo before age 13.

Folk gave way to bluegrass and, in 1962, led to his first professional gig as banjo player for San Diego favourites The Scottsville Squirrel Barkers whose mandolin player was a teenager named Chris Hillman. They recorded one album for Crown Records in 1963 entitled 'Bluegrass Favourites' which was sold primarily in local supermarkets. When the Leadon family once again relocated to Gainesville, Florida in 1964, the then 17-year-old Bernie was forced to give up the Squirrel Barkers.

For the next three years Bernie picked up jobs in a number of local bands and in the course of this apprenticeship he encountered future bandmate Don Felder. Leadon returned to Los Angeles in 1967, joining the folk-rock group Hearts And Flowers on banjo and guitar. This association lasted nine months; long enough for Leadon to appear on their second album, 'Of Old Horses, Kids And Forgotten Women', and to immerse himself in the growing but still largely informal music community.

Leadon left Hearts And Flowers in the summer of 1968 and was soon a regular in the spontaneous and, by all reports, legendary jam sessions involving former Byrd Gene Clark and Leadon's hero and ex-Dillards founder Doug Dillard. "Doug Dillard was always one of my idols," Leadon later recalled. "And those jam sessions were fantastic. We played music all day and all night for six months."

The jams ultimately turned into a formal band called Dillard and Clark whose début album, 'The Fantastic Expedition Of Dillard And Clark', was released on the LA based A&M label in October 1969. It failed to chart and seemed indicative of the band's shaky stature. Band members were constantly changing and, months before the album was released, the unsettled nature of the group was having its effect on Leadon. "I was getting bored," he remembered later. "The scene was getting too spaced out."

Leadon officially left the band in May 1969 (although he did get a credit as special picker on their second LP 'Through The Morning, Through The Night') and immediately found solace in Linda Ronstadt's backing band *circa* her 'Hand Sown, Hand Grown' period. But Leadon quickly developed itchy feet and, by May 1970, had hooked up with The Flying Burrito Brothers, the country rockers led by the charismatic, but ultimately doomed, Gram Parsons. His association with the Burritos, another revolving door situation, lasted through two albums, 1970's 'Burrito Deluxe' and 1971's 'The Flying Burrito Brothers' before he left in July 1971.

"When I left the Burritos, I felt I was a branch that had dropped off the tree to the ground until I could graft onto another one. When you leave a group, it's like you get it in your head to cast yourself back into the tank."

Leadon eventually found his way to Doug Weston's Troubadour Club, where he ran into some interesting faces.

"By that time," he says, "I had already started hanging around with Don and Glenn."

Randy Herman Meisner, the oldest of the original Eagles, came into the world on March 8, 1946, the son of sharecroppers from Scottsbluff, Nebraska, America's most central State. By his own estimation, Meisner was a kid "kind of out of the loop."

"I was kind of devilish," he says. "I got in trouble a lot. I would always take the dare. I was kind of stupid that way."

And, by virtue of his environment, he was admittedly shy. "I grew up in what a lot of people would consider a very passive environment. You don't see too many people on a farm and so I didn't grow up dealing with a lot of people. I was always unsure of myself so I usually ended up retreating. It was easier. I've always been passive and shy. I've never pushed myself on people."

Music ran in Meisner's family and so it came as little surprise when, at age nine, he made his singing début. "The first song I sang was at our school's PTA meeting. It was the Jimmy Rogers song, 'Honeycomb'. My parents got me this acoustic guitar at that point. I learned three chords and gave up formal lessons but I continued to perform at the PTA meetings, songs by Elvis Presley and Conway Twitty."

At age 14, Randy got his learner's permit to drive on the highway and began making the 10 mile trip from his parents' farm to Scottsbluff on a regular basis. It was through associations with townspeople that his first band, a Top Forty outfit called The Thunderbirds, came into being. A year later he was married with an infant son, not uncommon in the rural counties of America's south and midwest where too few job opportunities, isolation and a tendency to follow in father's footsteps conspire to keep teenagers at home and lead them into early marriages. But this didn't stall Meisner's musical ambitions and at 15 he made the switch from guitar to bass as he jumped to The Dynamics, a group started by his high school music teacher.

"The Dynamics started out as a Top Forty band but mutated into a rhythm and blues band which allowed me to do my James Brown thing," chuckled Meisner. "When The Beatles came out we went totally the other way and started doing stuff by The Dave Clark 5 and all the English groups."

In 1963 The Dynamics travelled to Denver to participate in a battle of the bands competition. They lost the battle but Meisner, in a musical sense, won the war. "There was this other band at the competition called

The Soul Survivors who had just lost their bass player. They heard me sing and I already had that really high voice that they liked. They were getting ready to go out to California and wanted me to come along. I said sure."

The Soul Survivors were Allen Kemp and Randy Naylor on guitars and Pat Shanahan on drums. Randy became their bassist and kissed his wife and son good-bye and headed with them to Los Angeles. There they joined a slew of bands in the emerging Southern California scene, living together in a tiny apartment and, later, in an equally small Laurel Canyon house. They played "a couple of shows" and discovered, much to Meisner's chagrin, that there was real competition in Los Angeles, unlike Denver where, according to Meisner, "one band could get all the local clubs wired up."

"We lost all our money and the house, then briefly struggled under the name of The North Serrano Blues Band. Then we got to thinking what would be a good name for the band. Well we were poor so we decided okay, The Poor."

The Poor released two singles on tiny Loma Records, 'Once Again' in 1966 and 'She's Got The Changes' in 1967. But the singles went nowhere, the band had to return to Denver on a regular basis to pay the rent and Meisner, in an effort to relieve the band's poverty stricken tradition, "had to sell my car because I was basically down to nothing."

About the time Meisner was handing over his pink slip, Buffalo Springfield were calling it quits and two of that group's roster, Richie Furay and Jim Messina were looking to form a country rock band. Meisner got wind of the gig and made his way up to Laurel Canyon to audition. As he was entering, future Eagle Timothy B. Schmit was leaving, having failed his audition to join what would ultimately become Poco.

Meisner auditioned and made the grade. Poco soon became a regular fixture at The Troubadour, the Hollywood folk club at the junction of Santa Monica and Doheney Boulevards that was changing with the times and giving bands like Poco and pre-Eagles projects like Longbranch Pennywhistle and Shiloh a place to hone their skills. It was soon to become the home of the entire Los Angeles soft rock movement, a place where those who would become its leading lights could share beers and swap dreams.

"We were all aware of each other but, at that point, I don't remember being real friendly with any of them. I knew Don and Glenn were starting to get together but the only real memory I have of that period was picking Glenn up hitchhiking once on Sunset Boulevard."

Frey has definite memories of Meisner; in particular of one night at The Troubadour when Poco took the stage. "Randy was like a ribbon. When I saw him, my tongue just fell right out on the table. I just couldn't believe that anybody could look, sing and play cool all at the same time. It was too much for me."

Poco began recording their first album, 'Pickin' Up The Pieces' in January 1969, but in the latter stages of that recording session Meisner was shown the door. "We had just started the mixing stage of the record and one day I called the studio when Richie and Jim were there. I said 'I want to come down and hear the final mixes'. Richie said 'Oh no, we can't let anybody down here when we're doing the mixes'. I said 'All I want to do is listen to what they did'. Then I told them 'If I can't come down and listen to the mixes, well that just isn't right'. They told me 'Well that's just the way it is.' I said 'Okay then I quit'."

Poco's response was to wipe Meisner's vocals off the record and his picture off the album cover. Adding insult to injury, the previously rejected Schmit was welcomed into the fold as Meisner's replacement. Needless to say, Randy Meisner was bummed. But a telephone call from Rick Nelson, one time teenage rocker in the process of converting to country, changed all that.

"Rick was looking to form a country rock band and wanted to know if I was interested," he remembers, "and I thought it was an opportunity to the guys who got me out here. So I got a hold of a couple of members of The Soul Survivors and we became The Stone Canyon Band."

Meisner and company supported Nelson on the live 'In Concert' LP released in 1970, and Meisner also landed a session gig on James Taylor's 'Sweet Baby James' album. Following the release of 'In Concert', Nelson took the band to Europe. but the steady diet of military bases and no home cooking was getting Meisner down.

"I wasn't making any money and I had been away from my family a long time and so I told Rick I couldn't handle this any more and decided to get out of music altogether."

He went back to Scottsbluff, Nebraska, and was relieved to discover that he still had a marriage. He took a job at the local John Deere tractor plant and settled into what he thought would be the straight life from that point on. But music for Meisner proved a magnet he couldn't ignore and he soon found himself playing nights in a local cover band called Gold Rush. "It was a frustrating time for me. The band would play until three in the morning and I would have to get up and be at work at eight. I started getting into work later and later."

Rick Nelson called again in 1971. "He was doing the 'Rudy The Fifth' album and he was having trouble getting the right bass part. I thought about it for a while and then went in to my boss at John Deere and told him 'this just isn't working'.

"Then I told my wife, I'm just going to go out there and try again."

Chapter III

In The City

Glenn Frey had barely entered the Los Angeles city limits when the myth of the City Of Angels appeared before him in a very personal and somewhat surrealistic manner.

"The whole vibe of LA hit me right off," he recalled. "The first day I got to LA I saw David Crosby sitting on the steps of the Country Store in Laurel Canyon, wearing the same hat and green leather bat cape he had worn on 'Turn, Turn, Turn'. To me that was an omen. Being in Los Angeles, I was a little bit intimidated, a little bit awed. But I got over that and decided that I would just try to make something out of my life in California.

"Almost as soon as I got to Los Angeles, I met J.D. (John David) Souther who was going with my girlfriend's sister. John David taught me how to play and sing country. We shared musical interests and we really hit it off."

Souther was also from Detroit and not too long after the pair struck up a friendship, they landed a publishing deal. "One of us got $40 a week and one of us got $50 a week," he recalls. "The deal, from the publisher's point of view, was that they hoped we'd turn in a few songs every couple of months. But they didn't like what we wrote. They would try to get us to write songs specifically for other people's sessions but, meanwhile, Glenn and I were smoking bongs of hash and writing these bizarre minor key songs about our experiences that were not even close to what these guys wanted."

While they failed miserably as in-house writers, they jelled musically, and under the name of Longbranch Pennywhistle landed a recording contract with an independent label called Amos Records.

Their album 'Longbranch Pennywhistle' was released in 1969 and while it went largely unheard in the real world it became a calling card among like-minded Southern California musicians. Among them was the raven-haired singer Linda Ronstadt, who'd arrived in Los Angeles from her native Arizona some years earlier and who, in the not too distant future, would figure prominently in The Eagles' chronology.

Frey and Souther celebrated the release of 'Longbranch Pennywhistle' by breaking up with their respective girlfriends and making the acquaintance of another struggling singer-songwriter, Jackson Browne, at a Los Angeles Free Clinic benefit concert. "He walked up to me and John David with an acoustic guitar and started singing 'Jamaica Say You Will' and we just started singing with him," said Frey.

Once again magic seemed to be in the air so when Browne suggested they all move into a broken down apartment complex in Echo Park, California to do their thing, Frey and Souther packed their bags. "Yeah, that house on Laguna St. was the place we lived at for a period of time," said Browne, smiling at the memory. "I lived in one of the upstairs apartments and Glenn and J.D. moved in next door. Then I got rid of the upstairs apartment because it would be $40 cheaper if I moved into the basement apartment below them. We became good friends pretty quickly because they were up there all night, every night, singing and so it was either grit your teeth or go up and sing with them."

The trio continued to co-habit in squalor that seemed to act as a lightning rod for the creative sparks between them. Frey and Souther, at one point, pitched in as backup musicians on Browne's demo tape of 'Jamaica Say You Will'. "The three of us would be living there," remembered Frey of the $60 a month rent and the good times. "We'd be listening to records or to Jackson practising his piano downstairs."

When Frey was not singing he could usually be found on the street, thumbing a ride to The Troubadour to hang out and draw inspiration. "I would do that about three or four times a week," he remembered. "I always managed to get a ride home."

Which was a constant source of amazement to Souther. "He had to be one of the best hitchhikers I've ever seen. I don't know how he did it. He would be standing out there in his fringed jacket and his long hair and all he had to do was stick out his thumb and somebody would hit the brakes."

In the wake of the 'Longbranch Pennywhistle' failure, Frey and Souther soon found themselves at odds with their record label. Some close to the situation claim the lack of a decent distribution system that prevented the album from even reaching the stores was to blame. Others point to a lack of a promotion and tour support. Whatever the reason, Frey and Souther wanted out of their contract and Amos would not budge. The result was that Frey and Souther decided to wait out the duration of the contract. The group, for all intents and purposes disbanded in 1970, and Souther and Frey went their separate musical ways.

"It was so frustrating," said Frey of the Amos Records incident. "I don't even like to talk about it. Everyday we'd go to the Amos Records office, ask if we could get released from our contracts and they would say no."

With time on his hands and few if any musical opportunities on the horizon, Glenn Frey started hanging out at The Troubadour.

David Geffen was not yet the empire building tycoon he would eventually become, but by 1970 he was certainly showing signs of the deft entrepreneurial skills which would bring him untold millions by the mid-Nineties. Asylum Records was yet to be launched but shrewd thinking and an uncanny ability to be in the right place at the right time had already taken him from the mailroom at a New York booking agency to the co-management of Joni Mitchell, Laura Nyro and Crosby, Stills, Nash and Young with his partner Elliot Roberts.

Into Geffen's hands fell Jackson Browne's demo tape, and he agreed to take on Browne and, at the singer's insistence, to informally advise Frey. Frey, with Longbranch Pennywhistle already history, was hot to get a solo career going. Geffen advised otherwise. "He told me point blank that I shouldn't make a record by myself at this point and that maybe I should join a band."

Kenny Rogers made good his promise to help Henley and Shiloh on their initial trip to Los Angeles in 1969, landed them a record deal with Amos Records, the same label that signed Longbranch Pennywhistle. Their first single, 'Jennifer', went nowhere but in later years Henley would recall that just being in Los Angeles helped ease the pain of a failed record.

"I remember driving into town. We came up the Hollywood Freeway," he told *Rolling Stone* in a fit of nostalgia. "It was a nice, clear February night, one of those nights when the town looks real pretty. I had never seen the Capitol Records Tower before and so I was freaking out. I was awe struck. It was like the town and the lights went on forever.

In the wake of their record's failure, Shiloh beat a hasty retreat back to Texas where new member Jerry Dale Surratt was killed when he rode his motorcycle into the path of an oncoming car. This tragedy, coupled with the lack of success their first trip to Los Angeles brought, sent the band into a temporary tailspin but they licked their wounds, replaced their fallen comrade and went into a two month woodshedding session before returning to Los Angeles to give stardom another shot.

With Rogers as producer and, for a short time manager, Shiloh went into the studio and recorded an album, entitled 'Shiloh', which was released on the Amos label in December 1970, along with a single with the title 'Simple Little Down Home Rock And Roll Love Song For Rosie'.

"It bombed too," said Henley. "It was a complete and total flop."

Shiloh, as dissatisfied with Amos's efforts as Frey and Souther had been before them, spent their time "sitting around broke and bummed out." But they managed some live performances that were definitely turning some heads.

"I remember one night at The Troubadour," said Linda Ronstadt. "I was on my way to the bathroom and this band Shiloh starts doing an exact version of 'Silver Threads And Golden Needles'. I was flabbergasted."

"But," winced Henley at the memory, "for the most part I was hanging out at The Troubadour, getting drunk a lot and getting ready to go back to Texas and call it quits."

On any given night Bernie Leadon could also be found at The Troubadour, drowning his frustrations in brew and casting around for a post-Burritos gig. So too could Randy Meisner who, after the recording of 'Rudy The Fifth' with Rick Nelson, was still dealing with frustration, financial insecurity and no small amount of homesickness for his family back in Nebraska.

"It was tough," said Meisner. "I was back in Los Angeles and things were starting to happen but, in a sense, it was just like it was before."

But if ever a place was suited for the tragedy and comedy that musicians, especially struggling musicians, bring to the table, it was The Troubadour. The club, located less than a block from the dividing line between Hollywood and Beverly Hills, had its roots steeped in the folk craze of the Fifties and early Sixties but, with the coming of psychedelia and the emerging rock and metal scenes, seemed out of date and in the way. But it was still a place where a growing community of unemployed, under employed and just plain rootless musicians might call home, hone their craft or, if lucky, land the gig of a lifetime.

"The Troubadour was the first place I went to when I got to LA," Henley fondly recalled. "I had heard about how legendary it was, and all the people who were performing there. The first night I walked in, I saw Graham Nash and Neil Young, and Linda Ronstadt was standing there in a little Daisy Mae dress. She was barefooted and scratching her ass. I thought 'I've made it. I'm here. I'm in heaven'."

Ronstadt, already in active transition from the early pop success of The Stone Poneys and well into her solo career, agreed. "We all used to sit in a corner of The Troubadour and dream. The Troubadour was like a café society. It was where everyone met, where everyone got to hear everyone else's act. It was where I made all my musical contacts, and found people who were sympathetic to the musical styles I wanted to explore."

And it was where Glenn Frey and Don Henley first got acquainted. Not that it was an easy get-together. Henley, by his own admittance, "didn't know anybody. I just hung around The Troubadour by myself. It was kind of pathetic."

His appearance initially rubbed Frey the wrong way. "I thought Don was just a fucked up little punk."

But one night Frey, whose initial negative impression of Henley had been fuelled by some fleeting conversations in the Amos Records offices, motioned Henley over to his table and, with a "What's going on?", extended a handshake and a beer. "I told him my whole trip was just stalled. I had all these songs and couldn't make a record, and I wanted to put a band together but I was going on the road with Linda. Henley said that he was fucked up too... we were both at impasses."

"Glenn and I had some conversations in the Amos Records offices but I really think we got to know each other at The Troubadour bar," recalled Henley. "Glenn was really charming and he was going somewhere. He had a fucking plan. He had a vision."

The conversations between Frey and Henley invariably ended up in gripe sessions centred around such complaints as "My group's not doing anything", "Things are a drag" or "Me and my partner are breaking up too." But during one Troubadour confab in the fall of 1970, Frey dropped a small bombshell on Henley.

"Glenn came up to me one night at The Troubadour and said 'My group is breaking up and I think yours is too. Do you want to go on the road with Linda Ronstadt and make $200 a week?' I said, 'That sounded good to me'" said Henley.

Frey was in the position to make the offer because Ronstadt's manager John Boylan was putting together a backing band for Ronstadt's upcoming 'Silk Purse' tour and rehearsals were due to start in two days. "We had been talking about drummers and Henley's name came up and the fact that he could sing was an extra bonus because Linda was doing a lot of songs with harmonies at the time," said Frey.

"I said 'Sure, fine, I'd love it'," said Henley, recalling his response. "I'd never really been on the road before."

As the conversation continued, Henley discovered an ulterior motive in Frey's offer. Glenn had taken Geffen's band suggestion very seriously and was not only scouring The Troubadour for Ronstadt but also for kindred spirits that would ultimately make up The Eagles.

41

"I told him I had all these songs and wanted to put a band together," said Frey.

As early as the rehearsals for the Ronstadt tour Frey had his ideas set in stone. "We had already started plotting and planning," said Henley. "He told me about Randy Meisner and Bernie Leadon and said we needed to get those guys because they could play the kind of country rock we were all interested in."

Linda Ronstadt and her band (initially the members of Shiloh, soon to be augmented by Leadon and Meisner) hit the road in the summer of 1971. "I got tougher being on the road with them," Rondstadt recalled. "I walked differently, I became more foul-mouthed. I mean, I swore so much that I sounded like a truck driver. I was the only girl in the band so the boys always kind of took charge. They were working for me, and yet it always seemed like I was working for them."

As for Frey and Henley, those early shows with Ronstadt pointed the way to a shining path. "It was like we knew almost immediately," said Frey. "The first night of the Ronstadt tour, we agreed to start our own band and immediately began hatching a plan to become what would eventually be known as The Eagles."

The Ronstadt band returned to Los Angeles after its initial series of dates. Another meeting at The Troubadour was held. Enter Randy Meisner. "We talked for a while and seemed to hit it off real well," said Meisner. "Both Glenn and Don felt that playing with Linda was a start in the right direction and a way to get things going."

Ronstadt was initially unsure about Meisner but agreed to let him join the band for a couple of San Jose California club dates. "We played the San Jose gig and it was fun," he says, "and I was really jazzed. It was clear that Linda didn't like my bass playing. She would look over at me and I would be rushing my playing. She was very conscious of her band's playing and so I could see immediately that I was a problem for her. But she did like my singing and that, coupled with the fact that she knew Glenn and Don liked me, sort of worked in my favour. But I was getting some really dirty looks from her during the set because I was taking some liberties with my playing. My attitude going in was 'Well, I'll play a couple of gigs with Linda Ronstadt'. But by the end of the night, I was so excited I remember walking over to Glenn and saying we ought to start a group. Glenn said 'Well that's kind of what we had in mind'. It turned out that Don and Glenn had the intention of playing with me and were kind of feeling me out... which I did not initially know."

Frey reported back to David Geffen who was trying to secure a record deal for Jackson Browne as well as taking an active interest in Frey's progress. "From the beginning I was encouraging Glenn to put a group together," Geffen once said. "Glenn would come to me with each new member."

John Boylan, too, was taking an interest, and some observers credit Linda Rondstadt's manager with recruiting Meisner and Bernie Leadon into the flock. For the record, history notes that Leadon was a drunk when he entered Don, Glenn and Randy's life in July 1971. During a Ronstadt show at Disneyland, the famous Southern California theme park, he staggered up on stage and began playing along with the band uninvited. Since no alcohol is ever served in Walt Disney's magical kingdom, this story seems as mythical as Snow White And The Seven Dwarfs.

"Glenn, Don and Randy had already begun sharing ideas and rehearsing," said Leadon later, which certainly confirms that he was the last to be recruited. "I tried it and I liked it. I was really impressed with the material that was presented. The song that I remember most was Frey's 'Most Of Us Are Sad', a very evocative song. The next day they decided they'd like to work with me, and we went... 'OK, we're a band'. The whole thing happened in two weeks. It was unbelievable."

With Leadon on board, The Eagles' line-up, to all intents and purposes, was complete. But Meisner recalls exerting some unexpected influence on Frey and Henley in heading off at least one more addition to the band. "At one point, J.D. Souther was almost in the group. I was the one who said no. I felt we had a good thing going with four people who really didn't know each other and that it might work against the group that Glenn and J.D. had been together before."

In August, 1971, Linda Ronstadt's backing band broke the news to Linda that they were going out on their own. "John (Boylan) and Linda gave us their blessing," said Henley. And with that blessing came the early, often uneasy, creative alliance between Glenn Frey and Don Henley. Frey, in particular, recalled that familiarity over a beer at The Troubadour did not necessarily translate into a comfortable working relationship.

"I would say our team was born a little bit out of desperation, a little bit out of fear and a little bit out of insecurity," he says. "Don and I, as individuals, had not written a lot of songs prior to the days of The Eagles and, all of a sudden, we were in a situation where we would have to learn."

But, as they began the early stages of their collaboration, in conjunction with Souther and Browne, Henley had to concede that the chemistry between them seemed to work. "Glenn had certain talents and personality traits that I didn't have. He was less inhibited and more brave about trying new things. Songwriting was new to me and I was a little bit shy. But he encouraged me and brought me out. He would just sit there with his guitar and do something, even if it was lousy, just to get things going."

Frey, Henley, Meisner and Leadon had an intense, two-week rehearsal period in a dollar an hour hall before presenting themselves to David Geffen. As well as honing their chops, there was a business-like defining of goals. "We had it all planned," said Frey. "We'd watched bands like Poco and The Burrito Brothers lose their initial momentum. We were determined not to make the same mistakes. We all felt that this was going to be our best shot. Everybody had to look good, sing good, play good and write good. We wanted it all. Peer respect. AM and FM success. Number one singles and albums, great music and a lot of money. I wanted to make it really bad. I was driven, a man possessed. In a sense I think we were all that way.

"We didn't just want to be another LA band."

Chapter IV

Meet The Eagles

Glenn Frey, Don Henley, Randy Meisner and Bernie Leadon marched into David Geffen's office at the Beverley Hills end of Sunset Boulevard, sat down and stared across the table at the up and coming rock mogul.

"Okay, here we are," said Leadon with characteristic bravado. "Do you want us or not?"

His brazen nature took Geffen by surprise. "Well... er, yeah," was all he could say.

It wasn't quite the Gunfight At The OK Corral, but it was pretty damned close.

"We walked in without a demo tape," chuckled Henley at the memory. "Geffen had no idea what we sounded like. It was a great moment. We all kind of sat there, wondering what would happen next and, finally, Geffen said yeah."

"Geffen may have had a deal in the works for us at that point but, at that point, we definitely did not have a deal," recalls Meisner.

There followed a stern lecture from Geffen on the need to stick together regardless of everything and anything. "Groups that split up never get anywhere," cautioned their putative manager with the wisdom of experience and the four musicians dutifully nodded. The meeting ended with a firm agreement by the still unnamed band that they would stay together for at least one year.

Leadon: "Geffen came down and heard it and he said, 'I'll do the deal for you on Atlantic if you want', or, 'I'm starting a management company that's going to be affiliated with Warner and my first artist is already signed, it's Joni Mitchell. And I've already signed Jackson Browne, so you guys can be the third artist if you want'. And he said, 'I won't give you any front money, but what I will do is give you support until you get a hit record, as much money as it takes, but we'll give you a stringent accountant and it's gonna be tight'. So we went for that."

Geffen then wasted no time in sorting out contractual matters, using his muscle and chequebook to clear up Frey's contract problems with Amos, buying up their publishing rights for $5,000 and giving half of the publishing back to them. "I believed in their talent," he said.

Geffen then fronted the band a reported $125,000 for an extended stay in Colorado where they could polish their act in the relative anonymity of small, out of the way clubs, well away from the prying eyes of Hollywood.

"Geffen just wanted to get us in front of people," said Meisner, "and he didn't want those people to be in Los Angeles."

Under the spoof name of Teen King and The Emergencies, The Eagles plied their trade first at The Gallery in Aspen, Colorado, and, later, at a joint called Tulagi in Boulder. They played whatever music came into their heads, whatever songs they knew from their pasts, and a few licks from songs that would one day sell millions of copies. They were simply playful, and there was no clue to the sound that would make them world famous.

"Everybody was just playing their own kind of way," said Meisner. "There was a lot of rocking kind of blues and a lot of cover songs. At the time we had started doing 'Witchy Woman' and we were doing a rhythm and blues flavoured version of 'Take It Easy' that was a real hoot. During that period we were playing three and four sets a night to sometimes nobody but the waitresses, drinking a lot of beer and just having a good time. But, as we played more, you could see we were getting tighter as a band and were using those gigs to boil down our song list to what really worked."

It was during the Colorado club days that veteran British producer-engineer Glyn Johns, who cut his teeth with The Rolling Stones and had lately produced The Who's masterpiece 'Who's Next', stopped in to take a look at the band. Johns was at the top of David Geffen's short list to guide The Eagles through their maiden recording experience and was checking out the band at his invitation.

"We were too much electric and not enough vocals for him," said Meisner of Johns' early impressions. "At that point, he decided he didn't want to have anything to do with us."

Frey, sarcastically, boiled the disagreement down to musical terms. "Glyn Johns was an Englishman who loved American country music and didn't think we could rock and roll. He used to say 'The Faces can rock and roll but not you guys'."

Johns, looking back on the night in question years later in the book *The Record Producers*, remembered his first meeting with The Eagles in great detail. "They were playing rock and roll, Chuck Berry, but sort of badly. You had Bernie Leadon on one side, a great country player, and Glenn Frey on the other, a rock and roller from Detroit, and they were pulling the rhythm section in two which wasn't very good at all. At that point they hadn't really defined themselves as a harmony band particularly well."

But the band learned fast, losing no time in settling on a defined style which would become their trademark element, the lush vocal harmonies that four distinct voices could provide. "After we got back to Los Angeles, we spent another three weeks just in vocal rehearsals," recalled Frey in a *Los Angeles Times* interview. "We were looking for a vocal stamp, something that when an Eagles song comes on the radio you know it's The Eagles when the harmony comes in. The same way you know it's The Beach Boys, The Beatles or the Stones."

While the boys were in Colorado and working on their trademark sound in Los Angeles, David Geffen was still casting around for a record contract for them and Jackson Browne. One day he was talking with Ahmet Ertegun, the founder and President of Atlantic Records, who was strangely reluctant to sign either of his clients to the Atlantic label. Then the conversation took a turn which would shape Geffen's destiny – and that of a whole stable of California soft rockers.

"You'll make millions with him (Browne)," said Geffen.

"You know what? I got millions," replied Ertegun. "Do you have millions?"

"No."

"Start a record company and you'll have millions."

"I thought 'Fuck him. I will start a record company'."

And so, in 1970, David Geffen formed Asylum Records for, at the time, the sole purpose of releasing Jackson Browne's début LP. As The Eagles project materialised it became a foregone conclusion that their first album would also be on Asylum.

Early in 1972, the band returned to Los Angeles and recorded a couple of demo tapes. They also began working at a small Los Angeles studio where a more laid-back, less electric state of mind took over. Glyn Johns, never the mellowest of men, found himself coming around to their style. "I liked them as people," he said, "which was the main thing that made me go back and listen to them when they got back to Los Angeles."

One night Johns came face to face with what he perceived as the essence of The Eagles. "I saw them in the studio, without the bad sound quality of the club and I realised their quality. It was just two acoustics and the four of them singing."

"We were just sitting around, playing acoustic," said Meisner. "And then one night Glyn Johns came in to give us another listen. We did about three songs and he came up to us and said 'Now this is what I wanted to hear'."

It was during this period that the band finally settled on the name The Eagles. Credit for the name rests primarily with Leadon, a well read and versed student of Hopi Indian mythology and lore. "In the Hopi mythology, the eagle is considered a most sacred animal," said Leadon. "It symbolises the highest spirituality and morals. I would hope that the music would soar that high.

"We all wanted a name that was short and concise, with an image, and we were aware that a name is what you make of it. I wanted a name with some imagery. Everybody was reading Castenada then and we wanted a name that would have mythological connotations. Frey wanted a name that could have been a Detroit street gang and Henley was sort of going along with the Indian vibe and all that, and everybody wanted a name that was just tough... Hey we're the fuckin' Eagles man! There was definitely a West Side Story aspect to it... We're fuckin' Jets, you know.

We're the fuckin' Eagles. Kiss my ass! So that went down well and we were The Eagles within a month of starting."

Henley and Frey began writing together in earnest, often collaborating with Souther and Browne. "Writing with those guys had all the great elements of classic collaboration," recalled Souther. "It was a very protracted process. We were slow, slow as molasses. Glenn would be walking around with a cigarette hanging out of his mouth, banging on a piano and keeping a groove going while Don and I tore our hair out and criticised everything."

Browne claimed that the atmosphere during those early sessions resembled *The Odd Couple* with, respectively, Frey and Henley as Neil Simon's characters Oscar and Felix. "Glenn was this mercurial sort of flash. He had boundless energy. Don was into being very analytical and methodical. He had the patience and the desire to hammer these songs into exactly what he meant them to be. They made a really good combination."

Frey agreed with Browne's assessment. "We had me, this guy with a million chords. I would go 'Well what about this or maybe you like this one.' And then Don would step in... who was real bright and had a good word and story sense."

Although he only knew them personally for a short period of time, John Boylan, Linda Ronstadt's producer, (who without realising it brought The Eagles together), saw interesting checks and balances between Frey and Henley. "Henley was the kind of guy you could count on to show up on time. All his bills were paid on time and his house was pretty much together. His symbiosis with Frey was based on difference. Glenn brought Henley a sense of fun and commerciality and Henley brought Glenn a more serious, intelligent, poetic way of looking at things."

In April 1992, just as the chilly English winter was turning into a mild and – for The Eagles – more conducive spring, the band arrived in London to work at Olympic Studios with producer Johns. It was here in

Barnes, where the River Thames flows nearby, that Johns had worked with The Rolling Stones on 'Beggar's Banquet' and 'Let It Bleed' and where he'd co-produced 'Who's Next' with The Who. It was the same studio where, in a mere 30 hours in 1968, Jimmy Page had put together the first Led Zeppelin album while Johns worked the board.

On the face of it, the move to London and Olympic seemed illogical. The Eagles had little in common with the illustrious British bands who'd spent sleepless nights making classic rock in the same room. Recording an American sounding act in such a totally un-American environment seemed to make little sense, and the band themselves weren't thrilled with the idea either.

"It seemed unusual to us," said Meisner. "Glenn and I, in particular, didn't like it much at all. We were heavy into the party scene in Los Angeles and, over there, we didn't know anybody. But that was the whole idea... to get us away from the partying so we could get down to work."

It might have been spring in London but it was still cold and wet by Los Angeles standards. The Eagles led a fairly dreary existence on their first-ever trip to the English capital and it was made all the more cheerless by the Spartan schedule set up by Johns.

"They stuck us in this little apartment," reflected Henley. "They picked us up, took us to the studio, and then we'd go back to this little apartment and drink ourselves to sleep. Then we'd get up the next day and do it all over again."

Johns and the band were in agreement that The Eagles, according to Frey, "should not make another limp wristed LA country rock album" and so, in a marathon three-week session, they set about making a country-rock album with grit. Meisner closely observed John's technical approach to getting The Eagles' sound on vinyl.

"Glyn very much wanted a live sound and so he miked up the drums and all the amps and worked with the sound as we were playing until it was literally live in the studio rather than incorporating a lot of overdubbing."

But Johns was the first to admit that disagreement and a war of wills was the order of the day in recording that first album. "Glenn and I fought like cat and dog all the time. We never liked each other much and I think a lot of that had to do with the fact that I refused to accept him as the leader of the band."

Henley, with due respect to Johns, saw things differently when he looked back in 1991. "The sound he was creating for us wasn't powerful. Glyn had this image of us as a ballad group. He didn't want us to rock and roll and he didn't think we *could* rock and roll. I mean he told us we couldn't play rock and roll and that we should forget it.

"He was a complete tyrant. We were really young and green and he just lorded it over us. He would give us three chances to do a track or a vocal and if that was the best we could do then that was it. And he had worked with all the heavies, so we really couldn't argue."

As the recording progressed Johns became a forceful teacher and the band was very often cast in the role of rebellious students. "He'd just stare at you with his big, strong, burning blue eyes and confront you with a man to man talk," said Henley. "You couldn't help but get emotional. We even cried a couple of times."

The often uneasy relationship between Johns and The Eagles was never more tense than when the producer's anti-drug stance in the studio ran afoul of the band's easy hand with marijuana, then the staple diet of California's music scene. "Every once in a while, Glenn and I would sneak out of the studio and smoke a little hash," recalled Meisner. "We knew Don didn't appreciate that and Glyn really didn't appreciate that. We respected that so we'd go outside, do it and then come back in. Bernie would sometimes smoke a little and he and I would get into Tequila and beer and just do that macho thing."

Johns claimed that he made The Eagles' début album with a very clear idea of the sound he wanted to get with them and the way he wanted to do it. "At the time they didn't seem to be overly enamoured of what was going on. In a sense I don't think they knew what was going on when we were recording that album. But I knew, and I don't think I was as excited [about an act] since I worked with Led Zeppelin. They were amazing but they didn't really know what they had at that point. I remembered when we finished it and were playing it back, they weren't jumping up and down. They actually didn't like the record very much until, of course, it became successful."

Although the band was constantly at odds with Johns, the relationship between the four of them was strong and mutually supportive. "The band was getting along real well and had actually become real good friends," says Meisner.

The Eagles returned to Los Angeles in May and re-recorded one more song, 'Nightingale', because they were dissatisfied with their attempts to record it in London. The sessions were actually the most easy-going and diplomatic in their entire career: Frey and Henley had yet to emerge as the band's primary songwriting team which meant there were equal and mutually satisfying contributions and collaborations from Meisner, Leadon, Jackson Browne, Gene Clark, their friend Jack Tempchin, the veteran LA based singer/songwriter, as well as individual efforts from Frey and Henley.

But Meisner, who would somehow become the band's soothsayer (although this strange talent rarely endeared him to his colleagues), saw the obstacles that lay ahead even as 'The Eagles' neared its June 1972 release date. "I don't go along with everything they (Frey and Henley) do," he said. "And I don't agree with some of our images. I'm just shy and nervous about putting myself on the line. But Don and Glenn have it covered. They're used to doing that."

Frey, addressing Meisner's retiring nature, once said, "He just likes to sit back and do his thing and let Don and I shoot our mouths off and make fools out of ourselves."

Which is not to say that Meisner didn't speak up when something rubbed him up the wrong way and quite a bit rubbed him up wrong when The Eagles played live. He would complain long and loud about how the band would just go on stage and not move around much.

"I sometimes felt that they didn't know the difference between recording and playing live," he said. "They were too serious on stage, too meticulous and perfectionist. They were afraid to vary from a set thing or to make a mistake. It seemed like they had a real aversion to having fun, playing different licks and just stretching out. The way they do it, you can go home, put on the record, put their picture on the wall and have the same effect. To throw in some different licks and to jam once in a while was like a sin to them."

Critical response to The Eagles' début LP was mixed but largely positive. Writer Bud Scoppa, in his *Rolling Stone* review, praised the record as "right behind Jackson Browne's record as the best first album of the year." Robert Christgau, perhaps the most difficult US critic to please, wrote somewhat bafflingly in his (New York) *Village Voice* column that The Eagles were "Suave and synthetic. Brilliant but false, and not always brilliant."

When it came to praise, faint or otherwise, from fellow musicians, opinions were likewise mixed. It was session musician and future Henley collaborator Danny Kortchmar who captured the title for the most colourful critique when, years later while working with Henley, he was asked what he thought of the early Eagles' songs.

"When 'The Eagles' first came out, I thought they were absolutely appalling. I couldn't stand them. They were absolutely terrible! Especially things like 'Peaceful Easy Feeling' and 'Take It Easy'. Because what they were saying was exactly the opposite of what I wanted to hear and what was going on in my life. 'Peaceful Easy Feeling' was a song about walking down the road in Tucson, Arizona, got seven women on my mind. Here I was trying to keep my marriage together and this guy's got seven women on his mind! God! It sounded like they were having fun but I sure wasn't."

The album's cover designer, Gary Burden, was a friend of the band who would subliminally shape the image that The Eagles presented to the world. The cover shoot took place out in the California desert. "We met at the Troubador at one in the morning," recalls Leadon, "and just drank our faces off, smoked all the pot and dope we could find and went out in my Toyota jeep and somebody else's car and drove off to Joshua Tree. We arrived at four in the morning, before dawn, to the secret spot of all the old time dopers, way out in the back overlooking Palm Springs. They had this old barber's chair way at the top of the mountain... you could sit there and it was great. We carried some guitars and all the camera equipment in the middle of the night, stumbled up this fucking mountain... made a fire and a camp and began making peyote tea and trying to eat peyote without throwing up... and the peyote was starting to come on and keep us awake... gave you that acid-like speed effect... those pictures are well stoned."

Henley correctly sensed from the very beginning that The Eagles were going to be labelled a certain way and that they would have a hard time changing people's conception of them as time passed. "We were judged by our first work," he said. "Our early stuff was country rock and so we were immediately labelled a country rock band. We got put into that category and we filled that slot. I knew, no matter how much our music would change, we would never escape that category."

They also *looked* like an archetype country rock band from LA. All four *always* wore tight, flared, faded blue denim jeans and matching shirts or t-shirts, ripened cowboy boots, and scuffed brown leather jackets which they removed before going on stage. Frey and Meisner had very long straight hair, Henley and Felder unkempt curly hair. All four were around the same height and as skinny as bean-poles.

To a large extent the album was everything the band would spend years railing against. It was pure country rock with the emphasis on country. Producer Johns' image of the band as a mellow act was apparent in the well mannered, often lilting arrangements. With the obvious exception of 'Witchy Woman', the lack of a forceful lead guitarist is evident in most of the songs and often results in solos that are tentative rather than expressive. The Eagles' ability to co-exist with songwriters outside the core group was a positive sign, but in view of the hype surrounding the band's song writing abilities, the small number of Frey-Henley compositions is a disappointment. But overall, 'The Eagles' was a sold début.

During the perfunctory round of press interviews accompanying the release of the album, they had their own opinions about what they were trying to say with their music. "We're a synthesis of all the Sixties music that was involved in folk, country and rock and roll," concluded Leadon. "We're just a synthesis."

Frey was optimistic yet cautious in assessing The Eagles' first vinyl attempt. "We would not be disappointed if the record weren't a success. We liked the album, it's a statement of our backgrounds. The Eagles were conceived as a song oriented band. It doesn't matter how good we can play if we play a piece of material that is inferior."

"We were all really excited when that first album came out," enthused Meisner years later. "We really felt like we had something going here."

Record buyers tended to follow the mixed lead of the critics. During 33 weeks on the charts, the album peaked at No. 22. The first single, the Glenn Frey/Jackson Browne collaboration 'Take It Easy', became the first of a long string of easy paced, radio friendly hits, hitting the charts at No. 12. 'Witchy Woman', a choppy Leadon-Henley contribution, became the second hit single off the album and the first to crack the Top 10, peaking at No. 9. The third single, 'Peaceful Easy Feeling', another mellow song in the same vein as 'Take It Easy' and written by Jack Tempchin, closed 1972's chart action by reaching No. 22.

"It wasn't a planned move that we record an album full of singles," said Frey. "But we did set out to record 10 good songs."

While their début album was chalking up respectable sales, the band was far from idle. They picked up opening act slots on bits and pieces of tours with an unlikely group of headliners, including the British acts Procol Harum, Jethro Tull, Joe Cocker and Yes. In hindsight, especially in the Nineties, it seems fairly ludicrous that a rock promoter might stick a band like The Eagles on the same bill as a soul belter like Joe Cocker or progressive rock symphonic merchants like Yes, but in the early Seventies rock had yet to become as compartmentalised as it did two decades later, and fans seemed far more prepared to appreciate its many and varied styles. "There was always the question of how we would go down with those kinds of bands but we always seemed to get a good response," recalls Meisner.

The 1972 tours were nevertheless a trial by fire, as The Eagles trotted out tentative selections from their first album, including 'Take It Easy', 'Peaceful Easy Feeling' and the more up-tempo 'Witchy Woman' and 'Early Bird'. Inevitably some audiences expressed collective boredom as they waited for more progressive headliners but such is life when nobody knows your name.

Frey would look back on those early tours as integral in getting The Eagles' collective minds heading in the same direction. "We realised that we weren't The Beatles. We realised that it wasn't mass hysteria and then we started to cool out. 'Take It Easy' would be the seventh song in a nine song set and no-one would pay any attention to the first six. Then we'd do 'Take It Easy' and people would say 'Oh yeah, that's who they are.' It's then that you realise that longevity and keeping your band together is what makes it, ultimately."

But life on the road for The Eagles during that first round of touring was not quite as serious as the corporate brains behind Eagles Inc. might have preferred. Apart from Meisner, all the band were single and eager to taste the libidinous excesses of road life, effectively the perks of the job for touring rock musicians.

"I was married at the time," reflected Meisner," but I was on the road and away from my wife and I fell off the wagon once or twice. Anybody who has been in my position and says they didn't is lying. It was very exciting to us because it was the first time any of us had been on the road to that extent and so we were a bunch of innocents. Travelling and touring was all new to us. We just didn't know."

As 1972 merged with 1973, individual band members took time out to work on albums by their friends in LA. Bernie Leadon's distinctive playing can be heard on Rita Coolidge's 'The Lady's Not For Sale'. Leadon, along with Don Henley, Randy Meisner and future Eagle Joe

Walsh, are all over 'Windfalls', the solo project of former Flying Burrito Brother Rick Roberts. Glenn Frey worked on the début LP of good buddy John David Souther and harmony singing is distinctly recognisable on David Blue's 'Nice Baby & The Angel'. Already, it seemed, The Eagles were making their mark on the LA music scene as a band and as individuals, and seemed destined for a successful and mighty long run.

But Frey was quick to sound a cautionary warning if anyone became too optimistic. "People have not decided to like us yet," he warned his colleagues.

Chapter V

It's Not Easy Being An Eagle

The success of The Eagles' first album, coupled with hit albums by Jackson Browne and Joni Mitchell, brought Geffen and his new Asylum label the millions that Ahmet Ertegun had promised. He capitalised on Asylum's early success by fishing for a buyer and finding one in Warner Communications, who purchased Asylum, lock, stock and talent roster for $7 million in 1972. Geffen stayed on as President.

In the meantime The Eagles, rather than making their follow-up to 'Eagles' more of the same, reverted to rebellious students once again with a proposal for a concept album called 'Desperado'. It was to be a series of songs that tied together the rise and fall of the infamous Wild West outlaws, the Dalton Gang, and it had its origins in a skull session between Frey, Henley, Souther, Browne and another local songwriter, Ned Doheney, in those pre-Eagles Echo Park days.

"We had a gunfighter's photo album in the house," recalled Frey of 'Desperado's' genesis, "and one night we just started writing a song about the Doolin' Dalton gang. We were going to do an all encompassing album about rebels or outlaws that didn't have a time reference. The Daltons would have sufficed for that entire period. We also started writing a song about James Dean that same night, the one that ended up on 'On The Border'. We also might have had some about Dillinger or Brando."

But when they became serious about doing 'Desperado', the all star-all era outlaw line-up was replaced by a concept that was 100% Old West. 'Desperado', in concept and design, was also a response to the band's initial success, and its sentiments were intended as a metaphor for the lifestyle of rock bands like themselves.

"The idea of doing 'Desperado' was a reaction to our initial success," recalled Henley in 1977. "We would have these conversations about whether we were just banging our heads against the wall, going up on stage and singing these songs. People seemed to want to see things that would take them away from their everyday lives. But our feeling was that you can escape too much."

There was an element of risk attached to ploughing ahead with a concept album so early in their career but Henley was unabashed. "That was the big difference between the first and second album," he told the *LA Times*. "The writing changed essentially because we were exposed, through our relationship with David Geffen and our exposure to writers like Jackson Browne, Joni Mitchell and Neil Young. We started looking more carefully at our own songs, almost as if they were pieces of furniture. Instead of saying 'that's good enough' after finishing a song, we'd spend a lot more time sanding the table top and varnishing it, working harder on the lyrics, changing one or two words."

Frey, that same year, was equally adamant about the importance of making 'Desperado'. "Let's face it, if you're a commercial success and that's all you are, that's a very vacuous existence. With 'Desperado' we had the artistic desperation, the story and the life signs."

Meisner recalls that Leadon and he were "all into it" but that the band pretty much stood alone against various forces that felt 'Desperado' was an unnecessary commercial risk. "It was definitely a bit of a risk," he says. "David Geffen wasn't too happy and the record company did not want the record at all. They were scared of it."

Fortunately, The Eagles had an important ally in Glyn Johns who liked the idea and again agreed to produce, and it was probably Johns' support that won the day, but as they went into songwriting mode for 'Desperado', it was starting to become obvious to all concerned that, to a very large extent, Frey and Henley were now running the show.

As early as the 'Eagles' sessions, Johns had noticed that Frey, although the youngest, was becoming the dominant character in the quartet. "Frey had his direction for the band while the others felt they were being squashed," he said.

"Glenn and Don were emerging as the key players at that point," said Meisner. "I just didn't realise it at the time. My whole idea was that I was a partner in the group and that I wanted to do what was best for all of us. But I was starting to feel like I was being taken advantage of.

By the time we started working on 'Desperado', Bernie and I were kind of on the outside.

"Don and Glenn had already started working on the idea by the time Bernie and I got in. By the time Bernie and I started thinking about what kind of songs we should be writing, we were being told what we should write by Don and Glenn. It was like every area I would start writing in for 'Desperado', Don or Glenn would tell me 'Well, we've already covered that.' They pretty much had the picture of 'Desperado' in their mind."

Meisner can recall one incident when the rivalries within the band seemed to rear their head. "Don and I were in a dressing room and I was playing around with my guitar and I picked out the first three chords of what would be the song 'Desperado'. Henley turned on me in a threatening manner and said 'If you don't do something with that, I'm going to.' I thought 'Why would he threaten me? Why wouldn't he say 'That's kind of neat.' But by that time Henley was only writing with Glenn and J.D. and so he had no interest in writing with me or even acknowledging my contributions."

Henley addressed the growing division in the band in 1975 by stating: "We've (Frey and Henley) just taken it upon ourselves that this is our department. We recognise that those guys have got a need to say something and if we can help them say it better, then I think everybody's better off."

The Eagles and Glyn Johns returned to London early in 1973 to record 'Desperado', this time eschewing Olympic in Barnes for the equally popular Island Studios attached to the label's offices on Basing Street in Notting Hill Gate. How the four week sessions went depended on who was in what frame of mind at any given moment. Meisner recalls that, given the pressure packed buildup, "the recording did not go too bad."

Frey, in an unexpected burst of praise during the 'Desperado' recording session, claimed: "Johns is invaluable to our records. He's just it. He's the one. We'd go anywhere to work with him."

But all was not sweetness and light. Johns, despite his support for the project, continued to do battle with Frey and Henley over their tendency to polish songs and constantly rewrite lyrics. Henley would respond with the band's trademark "no stinkers" philosophy. "When somebody hears a bad song, they're not going to say 'So and so wrote a weak song.' They're going to say, 'There's a shitty song on an Eagles album' and that reflects on everybody."

The band continued to complain about the cloistered lifestyle they were obliged to lead in London. Frey, in particular, disliked... "getting up, spending the entire day in the studio, going back to that sonovabitching flat, going to sleep, getting up the next morning and doing the whole thing all over again."

But Meisner corrects the notion that the band were virtual prisoners during the 'Desperado' sessions. "Glenn and I would hit these little after hours clubs and we always had an ice chest full of beer in the studio. We still managed to have a good time. But this was London so drugs were out. Things could be pretty dangerous at the time so we didn't want to play around over there."

'Desperado', at least in the minds of the band members, turned a corner about half way through the session. "Halfway through, we realised it was holding together," related Frey. "The whole thread between outlaw and rock star that we were trying to get across with the album was working."

'Desperado' was completed on time – one possible virtue of recording 6,000 miles away from home – and released on April 17, 1973. Reviewers, by and large, acknowledged The Eagles for risking a concept album at this point in their career and, for the most part, seemed to understand the whole cowboy-rock star point. Hollywood also came a-calling in the guise of famed Hollywood tough guy director Sam Peckinpah who optioned the album's storyline for the big screen (although nothing ever came of the proposal).

Unfortunately, although in years to come it would ultimately achieve platinum status, 'Desperado' was initially a dismal commercial failure, peaking at No.41 in the US album charts. 'Tequila Sunrise', the first single, only reached No.64, while the follow-up, 'Outlaw Man', peaked at No.59.

A classic example of being too hip for the room, this truly inspired concept album failed in a commercial sense but was a near seemless exercise from an artistic point of view. The band's confidence in the viability of 'Desperado' resulted in some classic soft rock, notably the title track, 'Tequila Sunrise' and the sadly overlooked 'Outlaw Man'. Johns, to his credit, released the country reins a notch or two and allowed the band to rock a shade tougher. The Frey-Henley influence on the direction of the band was beginning to solidify but, in terms of songwriting, the band were not yet ready to go it alone. But 'Desperado' was a sure sign that The Eagles could look forward to greater things in the future.

There was much gnashing of teeth in The Eagles' eyrie, and David Geffen was held largely responsible for the album's failure. Asylum was merging with Elektra Records at the time of its release and Geffen, soon to become the head of the new combined label, was heavily involved and unable to ensure that 'Desperado' received an adequate promotional push. In addition, Asylum – effectively Geffen – was on the verge of poaching Bob Dylan from Columbia where he had been since the start of his career, a massive coup by any standards. It was evident to all that although David Geffen was becoming enormously powerful in the US record industry, he didn't have the time to be The Eagles' full time manager as well.

"The record company was not on the case," said Johns, always ready to speak his mind. "Geffen had just taken over at Elektra and was more involved in trying to sign Dylan than putting any kind of support behind the album. It's disgraceful that it wasn't a monster hit album. It should have taken the world by storm."

Looking back on 'Desperado' in later years, Felder declared that... "I still think 'Desperado' is one of the most overlooked pieces of music to this day."

At the time of its release, according to Meisner, the band took it all in its stride. "I don't think there were any kind of feelings in the band that 'Gosh! We did the wrong thing.' It was like 'Okay, let's go on and do the next one now'."

In the meantime, a change of management was clearly needed. David Geffen, realising that he was stretching himself too far, gracefully stepped aside, preparing the way for Irving Azoff, whose stocky, often bearded, 5' 3" frame earned him the nickname of 'Your shortness' by the members of the band. What he lacked in stature he made up in energy and nerve, and his unstinting efforts on behalf of The Eagles would see them soar to great heights indeed. In time he would also become a major player in the American record industry.

Azoff, a take-no-prisoners *Wunderkind* by his early twenties, had been a fan of The Eagles before he came to work for David Geffen and his partner Elliot Roberts' management firm in 1972. "One day I had driven out to Claremont College [about 50 miles south of Los Angeles] to see them play," related Azoff, "and they really blew me away. They were my absolute favourite band. I had never met them, didn't know them."

Not long after he began working for Geffen, Azoff had a baptism of fire. "I was in the office one day and the secretary tells me I have to take a call from this raving madman, Glenn Frey. It turns out that The Eagles were leaving for the airport and they were upset because we didn't send limos. Elliot is sitting there, telling me he wants me to tell them to take a cab. So my first experience with The Eagles was being yelled at by Glenn for fifteen minutes on the phone about limos."

Once the yelling stopped, Azoff and The Eagles found that they had plenty in common. "We were all just a bunch of punk kids who were the same age. It was the first time I had ever been exposed to real rock stars. I immediately made The Eagles my business."

Geffen phased out of artist management as his presidency of Elektra-Asylum took up more and more of his time. Roberts stepped neatly into Geffen's shoes which, by ascension, left much of the trench work to number three man Azoff, which also meant he spent more and more time on the road with The Eagles. For Azoff, his early days on tour meant plenty of fun and games.

"Other than Bernie Leadon, who didn't think it was funny when I crashed into the back of his rental car, everybody thought that everything that was going on was hysterical," said Azoff. "The first three days on the road, I thought I had died and gone to heaven. These guys were out there with 400 girls."

The Eagles' relationship with Azoff would ebb and flow over the years and varied from member to member. Meisner, for one, was always suspicious. "He always seemed real nice but he was sneaky. You never knew what kind of a face he had on when he turned his back on you. I do know that he was always thinking money."

Frey, in a mid Seventies *Rolling Stone* interview, saw the diminutive Azoff in a different light. "I think it's great to have somebody pounding on record company desks and saying 'Fuck you! You're not getting another Eagles' album'. When we first met Irving, we had two gold records and $2,500 in the bank. Now we each make a half million every year and we see every penny."

Azoff's assessment of The Eagles at that point was nothing if not candid. "They were fabulous singers but not a great live stage performance. But the songs were very much on the cutting edge of what was going on."

Azoff's assumption of The Eagles' management coincided with the festering resentment between the band and their management firm over the lack of support for 'Desperado', and it would take a supreme effort on Azoff's part to rebuild the bridge. Eventually, he would form his own company, Front Line Management, and sever links completely with the Geffen-Roberts stable of artists, but before this happened all The Eagles felt a sense of rejection in favour of their other, better known and perhaps more prestigious clients like Joni Mitchell and Crosby, Stills, Nash & Young. "We were always the young guys down there," lamented Henley in 1975. "Nobody paid much attention to us."

The Eagles toured behind 'Desperado', headlining primarily at this stage and focusing on dates in the United States with occasional dips into Canada. As on the previous tour, the band, while never exactly monkish in their behaviour, managed to keep their road antics low profile.

"We always had our fun on the road," related Meisner, "but we never really took it over the line. We were a lot more gentle than most touring rock bands. It's not that nothing was going on. It's just that we respected each other's privacy. So, if anything was going on, we didn't necessarily know about it."

The band had risen a notch or two on the popularity poll and were able to play a slightly longer set that focused primarily on softer material like 'Peaceful Easy Feeling', 'Tequila Sunrise' and 'Desperado', but still included more robust songs like 'Witchy Woman' and 'Outlaw Man'. Their confidence in the 'Desperado' material was showcased in the band's 1973 Santa Monica Civic heading show in which they began the concert by playing the entire album in sequence, opening with 'Doolin' Dalton' and closing with the 'Doolin' Dalton-Desperado' reprise. It was greeted by thunderous applause.

Touring, like the writing process, was already shaping up as a battle of wills between the opposing points on The Eagles' compass. In particular, Meisner's laid-back demeanour was an ongoing source of irritation to Frey and Henley. "When we were performing, I always wanted them to be lit up front by bright lights but I just wanted to be in a blue light on the side," says Meisner. "They didn't like that. They wanted the whole band lit up and in front. I used to drive them crazy on that."

But Meisner acknowledges that his more demonstrative colleagues were instrumental in curing him of certain fears and bad habits. "I used to rush a lot on bass," he admits. "I'd get excited and the energy would start building and I'd play faster and faster which was messing up the band's overall sound. Henley was like a metronome when we were on stage. He taught me to slow down."

Frey pushed Meisner to improve his already ample singing skills. "I was there in the background trying to figure out if I could ever make it with my singing skills and then I would look at Glenn and see how he had improved. At first, he didn't sing in tune a lot of the time. But he developed into a good singer who was always on the money. I looked at the way he developed and figured I could too."

Following the 'Desperado' tour, the band made ready with no little reluctance to return to London again to record their third album under the continuing guidance of Glyn Johns. Once again the emphasis, according to Meisner, was to make "a commercial, monster album", but by now the creative differences between band and producer were widening at an alarming pace. "Glenn and I wanted more rock and roll out of it," remembers Meisner, "and Glyn Johns did not. He wanted more of the pretty vocals kind of thing."

These differences, coupled with growing internal conflicts and the band's general dislike of recording in London (again at Island Studios), made for six weeks of grief which became an exercise in self destruction. "They weren't happy with each other, they weren't writing very prolifically and they were finding everything rather difficult," said Johns. "We had six weeks and, at the end of it, we hadn't gotten an awful lot done."

"Glenn and I were basically not getting along with Glyn as far as what we wanted to do," says Meisner. "Glenn was probably more upset about it than I was but, at the time, I know I felt we needed the bass in there a little more and a harder drum sound. Glyn just didn't want to do that. No punches were thrown but there was certainly plenty of bad feeling."

Although they might bicker amongst themselves, The Eagles put up a united front against Johns. Even the stoical Henley, the rock around which the band managed to hold together, felt slighted by what he saw as Glyn Johns' casual arrogance. "I remember I had just come back from the bathroom where I had done some dope and I walked up to Glyn and said 'Glyn, can't you make me sound like John Bonham?' And he looks down his nose at me and said 'You don't play like John Bonham.' I said 'Aw, I know but turn it up a little bit.' But when it came down to it, we'd end up recording everything the way he wanted it."

The in-fighting over direction and where the band felt they should be heading reached boiling point during the 'On The Border' sessions. "We just couldn't finish the album with Glyn," says Henley.

Leadon, too, could see the writing on the wall. "That was the beginning of my leaving," he says. "I stayed and stayed and stayed... but that was the beginning."

Johns and The Eagles celebrated the end of 1973 with a permanent split. Johns was even-handed about the decision. "We did have some success while I was producing them and they became enormously successful when I stopped producing them. But they had some hits with me and it wasn't a bad start, really," he said some years later.

The final sessions with Glyn Johns had been far from productive. The band returned to Los Angeles with just two songs to show from six weeks' work, 'You Never Cry Like A Lover' and 'The Best Of My Love', both powerful ballads, the latter a Frey showcase destined to play an important role in the future. But as the New Year rolled in they were in a quandary about how to go about finishing their third album.

In April 1974 Irving Azoff split with David Geffen and formed Front Line Management. In later years Geffen said he gave Azoff The Eagles as a going away present to get him started, while Azoff has often said that it was the encouragement of The Eagles and their willingness to trust him that gave him the impetus to start his own company in the first place. Before long Front Line would attract a number of clients, including the urbane Steely Dan, future Eagle Joe Walsh, singer songwriter Dan Fogelberg, AOR rockers REO Speedwagon and the tragic Minnie Riperton who would die from cancer before the end of the decade. But here, unlike at Geffen-Roberts, The Eagles would head the roster and have priority claim on the time and energy of the company's main man.

The first business of Front Line was to find a producer to pick up the pieces of the album that would become 'On The Border'. While the band hit the road for a series of concert dates to keep their chops up, Azoff cast around. On some dates The Eagles were supported by guitarist/singer Joe Walsh, and it was Walsh who inadvertently solved Azoff's most pressing problem.

"When you're on the road, you tend to listen to a lot of tapes," he recalled, "and one night I played them some tapes that Joe Walsh had been doing with the producer Bill Szymczyk. I said, 'You need to go back in with someone like Szymczyk, we need to hear more guitars."

The band listened hard to Walsh's breakthrough album 'The Smoker You Drink, The Player You Get', deliberated amongst themselves and eventually agreed. Returning to Los Angeles, they met with Szymczyk at a restaurant called Chuck's Steak House.

"We had the meeting and I told the band that there was only one condition on which I could do the album," recalled Szymczyk. "And that was that I must call Glyn (Johns) and ask permission from him to take over. So I called Glyn up and he said 'Of course mate. I don't like them any more anyway'."

Bill Szymczyk took The Eagles into The Record Plant in Los Angeles early in 1974, much in agreement with their more rock oriented goals. One of his first nods in that direction was to bring in a session guitarist who would impress the others so much that by the end of the sessions he became the fifth Eagle.

Don Felder was born on September 21, 1947, in Topanga, California, and thus became the first native Californian to wear The Eagles' wings. An old friend of Bernie Leadon's, he grew up in Gainesville, Florida, but like so many budding rock musicians returned to the West Coast to find work and, hopefully, fame. Like Randy Meisner, Felder was a laid-back, easy going chap who was more than willing to let others do the talking. Reaching musical maturity at a time when so many stars were in the making, it is little or no surprise that every time he turned around he was bumping into future mates.

At the age of 15, Felder, still in high school, was a member of The Continentals, one of the hottest bands in Gainesville. The other guitarist in the band was an ambitious fellow named Stephen Stills. When Stills left, he was replaced for a time by a very young Bernie Leadon. History also notes that Felder once gave guitar lessons to a very young Tom Petty.

Following graduation from High School in 1965, Felder continued to gig locally until he joined a jazz group called Flow. Flow migrated to New York where they came to the attention of jazz starmaker Creed Taylor who signed the band to his CTI Records and, in 1970, released their one and only album entitled 'Flow'. The Flow experience whet Felder's appetite for the big time and, in 1971, he moved to Los Angeles, became re-acquainted with his buddy Leadon and quickly became a hot session and touring guitarist, working with various former members of The Byrds and The Flying Burrito Brothers.

Like all in the cliquey Los Angeles circle of musicians and studio hands, Felder had heard plenty of stories about The Eagles' alleged internal problems. But, he recounted in 1975, nothing could prepare him for the first day he walked into The Record Plant to play his first official lick as an Eagle, an overdub on the song 'Already Gone'.

"I was blown away that a great band like The Eagles would ask me to join in with them," he recalled. "I was thinking 'This is terrific!' Then I got into the studio for 'On The Border'. Bernie was bouncing off the walls. Randy was threatening to quit every week. They had just fired their manager and their producer. I thought 'What have I done? Being in the studio was like walking around with a keg of dynamite on your back with the fuse lit and not knowing how long the fuse is."

Fortunately Felder, much like Meisner and Leadon, was a low profile kind of guy and seemed to fit in perfectly. "I enjoy being anonymous," Felder would tell *Rolling Stone* in 1979. "I spend my spare time with my wife and kids. Don and Glenn have no anchors like that and so they handle being the rock stars real well."

Felder would soon add the now familiar guitar part to the song 'Good Day In Hell' and was officially asked to join The Eagles the next day.

"Felder's playing put the extra punch we needed in the band," said Frey. "The softer side to our records and live shows was always real good but, especially live, our rock and roll stuff was a little weak. Felder really nails down the hard stuff. From the moment he walked into the studio, he just blew us away. It was just about the best guitar work we had ever heard."

Meisner, despite the festering internal pressures, insists 'On The Border' represented a positive creative change in the band. "With the first two albums we were still relative unknowns and so we were in a situation where we had to knock them out pretty fast. But with 'On The Border' it was like 'Shoot! We're doing well and we're making money.' And so we had the luxury of playing around and being able to do new things in the studio."

Szymczyk's memories of the 'On The Border' sessions have dimmed with age but he can recall a seemingly recurrent theme on the album. "There was a lot of stuff about dead heroes on the album ('My Man' and 'James Dean'). The album was recorded right in the middle of the Nixon era when everything going on in the world was real odd and the outlook wasn't real bright at the time."

But while the outside world was spinning crazy, Frey claimed that The Eagles emerged from those sessions with a jump-start to their erratic concept of being a band.

"'On The Border' is easily the best sounding recording we've ever made," he recalled in 1975. "We're starting to learn how to become recording artists which is different from learning how to become members of a band."

Meisner finds it difficult not to reflect on The Eagles' constant creative struggles but nevertheless agrees that 'On The Border' was the stage when the band... "was really starting to get good. From the beginning, there was a desire in this band to constantly top themselves. It was like when we were finishing one album, we were already working on another. But, with 'On The Border', I think the band had finally reached a real good creative place."

To all intents and purposes The Eagles hit their stride after dumping Johns as producer and adding Don Felder on the lions' share of the lead guitar duties. With the inclusion of the ballad 'Best Of My Love', 'On The Border' exemplified the commercial ballad and mid-tempo rock style that would become the group's stock in trade.

'On The Border' was released on March 22, 1974, and in a commercial sense answered the doubts cast by 'Desperado'. It ultimately peaked at No. 17 on the charts and went gold within two months. Radio continued to treat The Eagles with caution, possibly because wrong decisions concerning which tracks to pull off the album as singles had been made in the past. The first, 'Already Gone', was a typical easy-going, country-rock Eagles' song with the sort of hook line-chorus that screamed AM rotation but it only reached number 32, while the follow up single, 'James Dean', a less likely contender for radio play, stalled at No. 77.

Reading the small print on 'On The Border' revealed that The Eagles were still an equal opportunity outfit when it came to songwriting. There were the Frey-Henley compositions ('Good Day In Hell' and 'James Dean'), a Frey-Henley-Souther tune ('The Best Of My Love'), Leadon's contribution ('My Man'), Meisner's 'Is It True?' and contributions from such outside songwriting sources as Jack Tempchin and Bob Strandlund ('Already Gone'), Paul Craft ('Midnight Flyer') and Tom Waits ('Ol' 55').

Souther, in particular, continued to be the unofficial Eagle. He never played with the band but Frey was quick to acknowledge his value to them. "He's given all his best songs away. He would start things and we would finish them. When we would bog down we could always call him because he's always been an inspiration."

Frey, ever prone to being cryptic, summed up 'On The Border' shortly after its release. "The new album is almost like life and death in

Hollywood. It's like a reporter's frame of reference. It's not an opinionated work as such. In the love songs, it's nobody's fault. Everything is just straight down the centre of the street."

The band toured behind 'On The Border' headlining more often than not at this point, or appearing at shows like the California Jam in which they played in front of an estimated 200,000 people, well up on the bill. True to Frey's predictions, the addition of Felder provided them with a sharper, tougher sound more suited to rock and roll and the bigger gigs they were playing. Like Meisner, newcomer Felder was married but the rest were all still single and they enjoyed the adulation and the women who seemed instantly drawn to the group's blue jeaned, silent, brooding *persona*. Meisner recalled that the strain of keeping his marriage together at such times was particularly acute.

"I was still married but, between recording and touring, things were starting to get pretty rough. I had brought my wife out from Nebraska a couple of times and we had bought a couple of houses. But she would get homesick, get fed up and eventually she would move back to Nebraska."

While Meisner's personal life suffered, The Eagles found themselves finally rounding into shape as stage performers. All bands that play together often enough will eventually get good at it, no matter what few resources they may have started out with, and the talent in The Eagles, now augmented by a skilled and experienced instrumentalist like Don Felder, blossomed in concert at last. While they would never aspire to the stagecraft of harder edged rivals, their confidence was high and playing on stage became easy. "We were starting to move around a little bit more in '74," recalls Meisner, always a bit of a shrinking violet beneath the spotlights. "We were finally starting to have a bit of fun."

This was an understatement according to Frey who chronicled The Eagles' excesses with glee. "We went on the road, got crazy, got drunk, got high, had girls, played music and made money," he said in 1975, sounding for all the world like a child on Christmas morning who cannot quite believe his luck,

But the fun was collared by the occasional blowups, especially by the road weary Leadon, and the more frequent emotional lows that are part and parcel of life on the road. Coming down from his earlier high, Frey acknowledged that problem too. "We've been lucky in the sense that, anytime anybody has gone off, there has usually been at least three guys who had it together that day. As long as we had at least three guys, we knew the shows would go and the work would go."

But all the discipline in the world couldn't stop Leadon whose doubts during the aborted 'On the Border' sessions in London were now turning into tangible dissatisfaction. "I was enjoying it... it was fun, but the reason I had to leave was the touring kept going on and on. Tensions between me and Henley and Frey were unnecessary – everybody was getting some money and there was no reason to compromise. And in the beginning there were no drugs. The pressure of the whole thing was really starting to wear on me. I was really depressed about my music – that was just personal – and my non-acceptance in the band. I felt we could expand in some other areas because we were so successful. The other guys were being very strong willed about the way they wanted to do things. So I decided to do it."

The signs were there for all to see, and not just behind the locked doors of hotel rooms or windowless recording studios. Leadon made a scene in a Holiday Inn coffee shop the morning after the last date of the 1974 tour, and the incident found its way into the pages of *Crawdaddy* magazine. "Perhaps the waitress forgot to bring the cream for his coffee," wrote their correspondent. "Overcome with exhaustion, depression and confusion, Leadon began yelling, raving, screaming."

As if The Eagles' recording and touring schedule was not hectic enough, during 1974 individual members somehow found the time to appear on albums by a host of other artists. Henley, Frey and Leadon sang backup on Randy Newman's album 'Good Old Boys'. Henley added harmony support to Jackson Browne's 'Late For The Sky'. Henley, Frey and Meisner played and sang on Dan Fogelberg's LP 'Souvenirs', Frey and Henley sang on Joe Walsh's 'So What' and, indulging in a little bit of pay back, Frey and Henley played on the tune 'You Can Close Your Eyes', a cut off Linda Ronstadt's critically acclaimed breakthrough LP 'Heart Like A Wheel'.

Commercially the band continued to be at odds with itself. Despite the fact that their more up tempo songs were going nowhere on the charts or radio, The Eagles continued to think of themselves as a rock and roll band. None of them felt that to release a ballad as a single would lift them to the Premier Division in the rock and roll leagues.

Finally, however, the band relented and, in November 1974, nine months after the release of 'On The Border', a third single, 'The Best Of My Love', was released. The Eagles didn't know it at the time but the leftover track from the aborted Glyn Johns' sessions was about to change their lives forever.

Chapter VI

Hello Hits, Bye Bye Bernie

Over Christmas and New Year, as California enjoyed a balmy holiday season and the rest of America shivered, 'The Best Of My Love', with its lilting harmonies and syrupy country-rock backing, captured that heretofore impossible dream for The Eagles, the AM radio, Top 40 listener. Early in the New Year it reached the coveted No. 1 spot in the *Billboard* Hot 100. Coinciding as it did with The Eagles preparing to once again enter The Record Plant with producer Szymczyk for their fourth album, its success should have been a sign to heavy up on the ballads.

But according to Szymczyk, this was the last thing the band wanted. "We were looking to go further and further away from the country rock influence and more towards a rock and roll influence. And we were looking at it as being a little more electric. I'd like to think I saw through The Eagles as far as their acoustic, cowboy elements went. I saw rockers who were dying and screaming to get out and I think I helped them."

He had also come to realise that Frey and Henley had already set in place a particularly high standard of playing, singing and songwriting. "Henley was always the English Lit. major. The final lyrics always seemed to be his. Until he pronounced the words done, they weren't done."

Frey, looking at those years in 1995, saw Henley and his songwriting chores as even more clearly defined. "I was kind of the McCartney to Don's Lennon. Don was more topical while I was a little bit more easygoing. I was the one more apt to sit down and write a love song while Don was more apt to chew somebody off. But, even though Don was always portrayed as the serious guy, I know for a fact that he also had a great sense of humour."

Szymczyk recalled that the 'One Of These Nights' sessions went on far longer than those for any of the previous Eagles' albums and would eventually clock in at a hefty six months, abnormally long for the time. Even the success of 'The Best Of My Love' – and the not unnatural record company pressure to come up with a follow-up as quickly as possible –

did not induce them to speed things up. The producer, who conceded that he could be rather slow on occasion, refused to take the blame. "In the case of The Eagles, I would say, a lot of it wasn't my fault. All of a sudden The Eagles were starting to take up an awful lot of my time," he recalled.

Felder, looking back on those sessions and, in a sense pointing the way toward future recording log jams, remarked, "We just kept pushing the bar up a few notches every time. We had to surpass ourselves and it all had to be greater than what had come before. Every detail on every guitar line, drum beat and background vocal had to be pushed to the maximum."

"The main reason it's taking us longer to do every album is that we just don't have the kind of time to collect ideas any more," said Frey. "We had 20 years to work on the first album and now the media wants something new every six months."

Henley stated the case for the band rather more succinctly. "This is not a high school game anymore," he told anyone who asked. "It's a fucking business... an occupation. It's a profession and it's fucking hard."

One of the reasons for the songwriting block that plagued the 'One Of These Nights' sessions was the fact that J.D. Souther, who in the past could always be relied upon to jump-start a writing session, had temporarily put aside a commercially unsuccessful solo career and, at the suggestion of David Geffen, joined up with Chris Hillman and Richie Furay in The Souther, Hillman, Furay Band. Consequently the unofficial Eagle was busy elsewhere.

In addition to this inconvenience, there were still old sores gnawing away within the band. Although Meisner insists that Frey and Henley were not taking the lead on the 'One Of These Nights' sessions, it was apparent that most of the songs that made the final cut during pre-production rehearsals had Frey and Henley's fingerprints all over them. There was also a growing rivalry between the two solo guitarists, Bernie Leadon, who had yet to jump ship completely, and newcomer Don Felder.

"There was definitely a little jealousy going on with Bernie about Felder being in the group," says Meisner. "Bernie wanted to play more electric guitar but the reality was that he was a killer acoustic player and a good electric player. Personally I thought Felder was tighter than a snare drum, but he is a great player and, in a way, I think Bernie knew that too. But there was just something between Felder and him that just did not blend in. So there was definitely some friction."

Henley agreed that the problems between Leadon and Felder were more musical than personal. "Bernie had his bluegrass roots so he never really understood how to get that dirty rock and roll sound," he says.

Felder, ever the master of the low profile, was able to avoid most of the squabbling by simply ignoring it, concentrating instead on the music. "I just recorded a lot of tracks in my home studio and gave Glenn and Don each a 90-minute cassette to work with," he told *Rolling Stone*. "No vocals, just music, because sometimes they needed a scene to paint their lyrics on. I knew the other stuff was going on, but I just couldn't be political."

Adding fuel to the fire was Leadon's personal life. Around the time of 'One Of These Nights' he began dating Patti Davis Reagan, the daughter of the soon to be President Of The United States, Ronald Reagan. In her autobiography *The Way I See It*, Patti revealed, somewhat presciently, that in 1974, just after 'On The Border' had been released, she was looking at the album insert and at the photo of Bernie Leadon and had a feeling that somehow she was going to meet him.

She was right. A few days later Reagan, then an aspiring songwriter, ran into Leadon at a West Los Angeles music store. A whirlwind romance blossomed between the pair and she was soon living with Leadon. She even accompanied The Eagles on their 1974 tour of Europe. "I didn't really notice it at first," she chronicled in her book, "but Bernie's relationship with the rest of the band was starting to fracture. I didn't know when I started letting Bernie see some of my songs that it would increase the tensions that already existed."

Reagan remembers that she wrote a song entitled 'I Give You Peace' at a time when The Eagles, and particularly Leadon, were having trouble coming up with anything they liked for the 'One Of These Nights' album. "I played him a song I had written called 'I Give You Peace' and he immediately wanted to help finish it and record it as a cut on the next LP. I knew the group had already made a decision not to use any more outside writers. But Bernie insisted that they make an exception to that rule. They agreed but I'm sure it didn't help his relationship with the rest of the band."

The extent of the strain Reagan's presence caused in The Eagles' circle is difficult to determine. "She was around," said Meisner, "and she started doing some songwriting with Bernie. Glenn and Don didn't care too much for it but I didn't have any problem with it. Bernie's relationship with Patti was not interfering with the band as far as I was concerned."

Henley saw things differently. "I sort of resented her being around at the time," he freely admitted in a 1989 *Musician* interview. "I thought she was butting in. She co-wrote one song with Bernie and he insisted the song go on the album. Nobody else wanted it. We didn't feel it was up to the band's standards. But we put it on anyway as a gesture to keep the band together. Then she did an interview (which ran in the *Las Vegas Sun*) in which she said 'I write songs for The Eagles'."

This was like a red rag to a bull as far as The Eagles' principal writers, Henley and Frey, were concerned. Henley became so incensed when the story appeared that he immediately fired off a letter to the editor of *The Sun* setting the record straight. Then he and Frey finally took this particular bull by the horns, retiring to a rented Hollywood mansion where they knocked out the majority of the songs destined for the album amid a pile of Tequila bottles and writing pads.

The recording of 'One Of These Nights' continued at a snail's pace. With the band becoming more withdrawn as the sessions progressed, and even less inclined to talk to the press than they normally were, it became manager Azoff's duty to answer the constant barrage of questions as to why The Eagles were not rushing to capitalise on their sudden commercial success. "There was a lot of give and take on that fourth album," Azoff told veteran music writer Irwin Stambler. "But I wouldn't call it fighting. It's a matter of rounding out, finishing off the rough edges. They feel an obligation to the music field to maintain quality. Even more than before, they all want to take their time."

If anybody benefited from the leisurely pace of 'One Of These Nights' it was Randy Meisner whose voice became the centrepiece of some of The Eagles' most recognisable songs, most notably his stunning falsetto at the climax to his own 'Take It To the Limit'. "On 'One Of These Nights' Randy found himself as a vocalist," Frey related in the late Seventies. "With songs like 'Take It To The Limit' and 'Too Many Hands' we felt we finally found the right songs for Randy to sing."

Meisner agreed. "I didn't get to shine too often with The Eagles but 'One Of These Nights' turned out to be a big album for me. I felt I really shone on the song 'One Of These Nights' and I was beaming on 'Take It To The Limit'."

Bill Szymczyk agreed. "Recording Randy's voice on that song ('Take It To The Limit') took a bit of time but I still consider it a showstopper song for the band. He's got a great voice and it was perfectly suited for that song."

The producer's main job was to act as a referee between Frey and Henley and the other three, especially Leadon who was inclined towards angry outbursts. Szymczyk recalled how one incident led to music history of sorts. "At the time Bernie had only one song on the album... this instrumental thing he wanted to do. Well nobody else in the band was in favour of it but I liked it so we worked on it, adding strings, backward guitar and some space sounds to the basic banjo track. The working title of the track was 'Fellini In Florida'. On the album the title was 'Journey Of The Sorcerer' and, years later, the song became the theme music to the British television series *The Hitch-Hiker's Guide To The Galaxy*."

But throwing what turned out to be creative bones in the direction of Leadon could not defuse the fact that he was losing interest at a rapid pace. "I can remember one incident in particular," related Szymczyk in *The Record Producers*. "We were listening to some of the tracks we had done the night before. Bernie was lying on a couch in front of the board and, because the rest of us were at the console, we really couldn't see him. We were trying to decide on which of a bunch of takes to use and everybody seemed to have an opinion. Finally I asked Bernie what he thought and he got off the couch and said 'I think I'm going surfing'. He got up, walked out of the studio and we didn't see him for three days."

Leadon came back in time for the official release of 'One Of These Nights' on June 10, 1975. Largely a Frey-Henley written album – six of the nine tracks carried their credit – 'One Of These Nights' also indicated that The Eagles had finally come to terms with the commercial flame lit by 'The Best Of My Love'. 'One Of These Nights' zoomed to the top of the pop album charts, going gold in a mere three weeks. The title track, the first single off the album, raced to No. 1 by the first week in August. The album's second single, 'Lyin' Eyes', would reach No. 2 in November and 'Take It To The Limit' would complete the hat trick with a No. 4 chart peak early in 1976.

The critics, again not unexpectedly, were quick to damn with faint praise. While generally appreciated for their songwriting, The Eagles took knocks for being the quintessential bland Seventies rock stars, relying too heavily on overtly commercial lyrics and a mannered, often overly orchestrated, sound. There was a continuing trend towards mellow shadings which exposed the need for a heavy duty rock guitarist besides Felder. Six of the nine tracks on the album are Frey-Henley collaborations and most of them were so radio friendly that they were impossible to ignore.

Henley's reply: "It's not a sin to be in the Top 40."

Neither was it a sin for Henley, when not bashing back at the critics, to wax philosophical about the just completed album and its contents.

"The music can be about anything. It can be about a woman, fame or peace of mind. What is important is how you feel about the prize once it is won."

The Eagles embarked almost immediately on a massive US tour in support of 'One Of These Nights', with headlining shows in arenas, sprinkled with a smattering of big outdoor events. Everybody connected with the band held their breath as the tour kicked off. It was only a matter of time before Leadon's dissatisfaction reached critical mass.

What they had not counted on was Leadon nearly blowing off the band and the tour before it even started. "The night before the tour, Bernie wrote up a will," remembered Patti Reagan. "He was supposed to be packing for the tour but he was just sitting there, talking about death by airplane and how if he got on the plane with the rest of the band the next morning he would die. Bernie had been thinking about leaving The Eagles for quite a while and so, with this fear all over him, it seemed as if right then was a good time to leave.

"So the next morning Bernie called up Irving Azoff and said he was not going on the tour. Everybody panicked. One of the lawyers for the band was already on his way up to the house to try and talk Bernie out of quitting. Finally we convinced Bernie that, if he thought this particular plane was going to crash, then he could follow the rest of the band on another plane the next day. Obviously neither plane crashed but Bernie, just to play it safe, rented a motor home and drove between concert dates on the East coast for a week before he decided that he could fly again."

Frey, in a 1976 interview, said, "We actually knew about a year and a half earlier that Bernie would be leaving the band at some point. We knew he wasn't happy touring. We knew he was gonna leave."

And the band, Frey explained in 1995, was already looking at Leadon's impending departure as a way of shoring up a long-standing weakness. "When The Eagles started out, we were a country rock band with the emphasis on country. When we went out on those early tours with bands like Jethro Tull and Yes, we were taking a beating out there. Don and

I kept visualising that we needed this kick ass segment to our live show, something at the end to just kind of take off with. We always felt that, even with Felder in the band, we needed a little more firepower."

However, in a *Rolling Stone* article just three months prior to his departure, Leadon seemed upbeat about The Eagles and his future in the band. "My attitude toward the band is pretty good these days," said Leadon. "We've all grown a lot. I think the music is worth something. There's some thought and living behind it."

Those good vibes, however, were countered by continued temper tantrums and outbursts which, recalled Meisner, resulted in a blowup in a hotel in the deep South as the US phase of a proposed world tour was grinding to its conclusion. "I kept talking to Bernie, trying to convince him to stick it out until the entire tour was over," reflected Meisner. "But this one night he just couldn't take it any more. Glenn was sitting in the hotel bar and, all of a sudden, Bernie walked in, picked up a beer, dumped it over Glenn's head and walked out. That was it. Bernie just quit."

Bernie Leadon officially left The Eagles on December 20, 1975. The official explanation for his departure was trotted out as his growing dissatisfaction with the band's musical direction. But Leadon, looking back on his decision in a 1979 *Rolling Stone* interview, claimed there was more to it than that.

"I kept asking, 'Are we going to rest next month?' and we never did. I wanted to get in shape before the age of 30 so I could have a chance at the rest of my life. I was afraid something inside of me was dying. Leaving was an act of survival."

At that point, recalled Meisner, The Eagles were left with the prospect of cancelling a long and lucrative European tour. But cancelling was not the band's style. "We just decided 'now was the time'," said Meisner, "and that's when Joe Walsh stepped in."

Chapter VII

The Last Day Of A Good Eagle

On the face of it Joe Walsh was an unlikely Eagle. A tough, wise-cracking, off-centre guitarist with a crazy glint in his eye, raggedy blond hair and droopy moustache, he didn't even look like an Eagle, much less sound like one when he cranked up his Les Paul and made noises not unlike the grunge that exploded out of Seattle in the Nineties. No lesser noise enthusiast than Pete Townshend was among his admirers, and if ever there was a rock star unlikely to sing the praises of the mellifluous Eagles, it was The Who's blunt speaking *major domo*. But Joe was recruited to add sour to the sweet, to bring with him his uncanny ability to hot-wire an electric guitar to make it sound like a flying saucer, and he stuck with The Eagles until the end of the flight.

He might have been born on November 20, 1947, in Wichita, Kansas. That's what the experts say. The conspiracy theorists opt for a 1945 birth in either Cleveland or New York City. What is beyond doubt is that by the time Walsh could mouth the word guitar, he was playing one. "I was young, real young when I started playing," recalled Walsh. "How young? I'm not sure but I think guitar and girls were a dead heat."

In typical Walsh fashion, the guitarist was a bit ahead of himself with that statement. Point of fact: Walsh got the musical urge after hearing his mother play classical piano. Through high school the oboe and clarinet were his instruments of choice followed by his first stringed instrument the bass.

Shortly after his birth, the Walsh family moved to New Jersey where teenage Joe began performing in the local bands G-Clefs and The Nomads. He half-heartedly enrolled at Kent State University in 1965. "I became the phantom of Kent State," he recalled. "I was taking electronics, music theory, welding... all these weird courses that nobody could understand."

Walsh hooked up with local Ohio faves The Measles that same year, but stayed at Kent State until 1968, just long enough to be an eye witness to history. "I remember standing on a hill," recalled the guitarist in 1980. "I heard the National Guard open fire and I saw the students on the ground. Two of the people who were shot were really good friends of mine. That whole thing at Kent State made me furious and I'm still furious."

Walsh managed to stick it out with The Measles until 1969 when he got a call from Cleveland to become the new guitarist in a power trio called The James Gang. The band, with Walsh unleashing his trademark screaming power leads, became the hot item in town, and one night a producer for ABC Records named Bill Szymczyk happened to be in the audience, liked what he saw and convinced his label to sign them up.

October, 1969, saw the release of The James Gang's début LP, 'Yer Album', which eventually rose to No. 83 on the *Billboard* album charts. Always fast workers, The James Gang raced back into the studio and, in July 1970, released 'James Gang Rides Again' which reached No. 20 and went gold, while the single 'Funk No. 49' topped out at No. 59. In the fall of 1970, they rushed out a third album, appropriately titled 'Thirds' which, likewise, went gold and produced two chart singles, 'Midnight Man' and the Walsh guitar volume feedback classic 'Walk Away'.

The James Gang's fourth album in two years, 'Live In Concert', came out in 1971 and went on to become the band's third consecutive Top 30 chart success. But Walsh, despite, or perhaps because of, his growing notoriety as a guitar slinger, bolted the band in November of that year. "I felt I was ready to go it alone," he said. "After I left The James Gang, I really thought I would emerge as Joe Walsh: Guitar Player."

Walsh moved to Colorado, formed a new trio called Barnstorm, and, early in 1972, released an album called 'Barnstorm' which, according to Walsh, "Dropped dead. Nothing happened." Undaunted, Walsh returned to the studio, working sporadically with producer Szymczyk, and emerged in 1973 with the album 'The Smoker You Drink, The Player You Get' which contained his greatest hit 'Rocky Mountain Way'. The album was an unexpected smash, rising to No. 6 on the *Billboard* charts and turning Walsh into a legitimate solo act. With various incarnations of a Barnstorm backing band, he toured extensively throughout 1973 and

1974 before returning to the studio late in 1974 to record a follow up album entitled 'So What' which was released early in 1975 and reached No. 11 on the charts. Was Walsh happy? Well, sort of.

"Joe wanted to be in a group," explained Henley in a post 'Hotel California' interview. "He was tired of hiring bands, tired of making decisions and tired of writing all the songs."

Years later, in a 1989 *Musician* interview, Henley would be even less delicate in describing what he perceived as Walsh's sagging fortunes. "His career was in really bad shape at the time. He wasn't getting anywhere."

Whatever Joe Walsh's personal state of mind and career prospects, the fact that he and The Eagles shared management, played together and seemed to be on the same philosophical and creative wavelength, made him the ideal choice to step into Leadon's shoes.

According to Frey, the decision to add Walsh was not made overnight, as it might have seemed, given the haste with which his recruitment was announced. "We had talked to Joe before Bernie left," reflected Frey in a 1976 *Melody Maker* interview. "And his attitude was if it happens (Bernie leaves) we should give him a call. By the time Bernie left we knew there was only one guitar player for The Eagles."

Producer Szymczyk, who was thought to have used his ties with Walsh to slide him into the band, denied he had anything to do with the move and was, in fact, lukewarm about the decision. "I had very little to do with it, and as a matter of fact, I was not a great fan of the move. Joe had his own career going very well at the time and I almost did not want to see him joining a group again. How it came about was strictly Joe and The Eagles getting together, hanging out and his being invited to join the band."

Walsh, for his part, seemed delighted with the outcome. "After a couple of albums by myself, I was starting to feel drained, alone and in need of feedback. I just did not want to have to keep rehearsing a band and putting out all these intense amounts of energy. And musically I felt I could relate to these other four guys."

Ten days after Bernie Leadon played his last gig with The Eagles came the announcement that Walsh had joined the band. Frey, in 1976, explained the reason for the quick announcement. "We didn't want the rumours to start. We didn't want people to start saying that Bernie had left the band and so that was it for The Eagles."

Henley recalls that the announcement was greeted not so much by shouts of The Eagles are breaking up so much as cries of 'Why Joe?' "Most of the media suggested that he wouldn't fit in because we were perceived as a much mellower band than anything he had ever been involved in." Admitting that he enjoyed the infusion of musical bite that Walsh brought to the band, Henley looked back in hindsight during a 1989 *Musician* interview with some misgivings. "I think Joe had the attitude at the time that he was doing us a favour. He was a little reluctant about it and I think he was almost ashamed of it for a while."

But once the band got down to rehearsing, it became evident that Walsh fitted in musically and otherwise with the rest of the group. "We were right in click when Joe came in," recalled Meisner. "We liked to party the same amount and play the same kind of jokes."

"I really liked playing with Joe," related Felder of those early days. "It was good to be able to bounce off somebody who could give back more than you sent out."

With Walsh road-ready, the band wasted no time in testing their latest member, taking off on a world tour that took in Japan, Australia and New Zealand. It was a time of inner turmoil, according to Don Felder. "We were breaking Joe in and doing the tour and we knew we'd have to do another album pretty soon. Just trying to get through everything was real tough and there was a real element of uncertainty about what was going to happen next."

The band's 1976 concert tours were tentative affairs designed primarily to work Walsh into the act and to relieve the pressure of recording 'Hotel California'. The Eagles performed the best known songs from their repertoire, now including 'One Of These Nights', 'Take It To The Limit', 'Best Of My Love' and 'Lyin' Eyes', as well as a couple of Joe Walsh' better known songs, 'Rocky Mountain Way' and 'Turn To Stone', which added a much needed punch to the set. Later that year, as 'Hotel California' neared its completion, audiences were treated to the first live performances of the title track, 'New Kid In Town' and 'Wasted Time'.

They faced the uncertainty head on in May, 1976, when The Eagles made their first US appearance with Walsh in the line-up at a big outdoor concert that also featured Linda Ronstadt and Jimmy Buffett. *Los Angeles Times* writer Robert Hilburn felt that Walsh was too conscious of the importance of the show and seemed to hang back, rarely doing leads and allowing Felder to handle most of the up front guitar work. But the prognosis was that once Walsh became more comfortable in the band, the harder element he would bring to The Eagles would be worth the wait.

Henley, speaking after the show, was nothing if not cautious about the band's immediate future. "We're a target now," he told Hilburn. "That's why we're working so hard on the new album. There are a lot of eyes watching. We had hoped to have it ready for the start of the tour but we may not be able to make it. It may have to come out during the tour instead. We just won't let it go until we're satisfied with it."

Back on the road, Walsh's musical impact was immediate. The band sounded tougher. Critics were starting to come around and, in many cases, the band was gaining a certain respect previously denied to them. But while things appeared calm and upbeat on the surface, Meisner, still feeling like the odd man out, was beginning to see the writing on the wall.

"I was getting real frustrated at the time because Don and Glenn had pretty much taken over the songwriting and just about everything else connected with the band," he says. "All the decisions were being made by them, and it's not that their decisions were bad... it was just the way they made them. It was like they would decide on things and then present them to the rest of us in a way that said 'Okay this is what we're going to do'."

Things weren't much better on the personal front either. "I got along with Don and Joe pretty well but Glenn and I were starting to not be as close as we once were. It had gotten to the point that Don and Glenn were so close that, all of a sudden, I wasn't in their click any more. I tried to be friends with Don but he was always real stiff."

Meisner's marriage was also pretty much on the rocks. "By then it seemed we were on the road all the time and everything we did was real extreme and real fast lane. At that point everybody in the band was into drugs and alcohol real bad."

Of greater concern to Elektra-Asylum was the fact that it was coming up on a year since the release of 'One Of These Nights' and The Eagles, or most importantly Frey and Henley, were showing no indication of getting songs together for their next album. The label wanted an Eagles' album out so badly that they went back to the vaults and, on February 17, 1976, they released 'Their Greatest Hits: 1971-1975'.

They had heard it all before but that did not stop Eagles' fans from snatching up the package in unbelievable numbers. 'Their Greatest Hits' went gold and platinum in its first week of release, topped the album sales charts for five weeks during March and April and finally ended up selling in excess of 12 million copies. It was almost to be expected that The Eagles were not amused.

Frey was actually surprised. "I never expected a greatest hits album to do five million. I mean the people who bought this already own all our albums." Henley, ever the cynic, grumbled "I've never been a fan of greatest hits albums. I feel they're more or less a ploy by the record company to get free sales."

Despite The Eagles' collective grousing about milking fans, the greatest hits collection was valid insofar as it brought to a close the first stage of their career, the pre-Joe Walsh period dominated by country rock.

A little more than a week after the release and monstrous success of 'Their Greatest Hits', The Eagles took a giant step toward critical favour when, on February 28, they captured the Grammy award for Best Pop

Vocal Performance by a group for the song 'Lyin' Eyes'. Also in February, Joe Walsh released a live solo album, 'You Can't Argue With A Sick Mind', which featured Felder on guitar and Frey and Henley on backup vocals on the song 'Help Me Make It Through The Night'. The album ultimately reached No. 20 on the album charts.

It was during the period after 'One Of These Nights' that The Eagles lived out the rock star lifestyle to the hilt. Meisner recalls that the band was split geographically, living many miles apart. "I was living out in Topanga Canyon and Don (Felder) was fairly close by. Don and Glenn were living in the city and pretty much living the Hollywood lifestyle you would expect them to be leading."

Henley was more specific in the book *Off The Record*: "We were basically dudes on a rampage. Glenn and I would go through a series of moving in together and then moving out. We'd have girlfriends and live with them for a while and then we'd get ready to do an album and we'd move back in together. It was funny the way we kept moving in, having girlfriends, breaking up and moving back in together.

"But it was like the music always came first and I think we wanted it that way," he continued. "We wanted to have relationships with women and have the band too."

For a while Henley enjoyed a relationship with Stevie Nicks, the singer with Fleetwood Mac who had finally ended her lengthy on/off affair with Fleetwood Mac's guitarist, Lindsey Buckingham.

In a 1976 interview with *Crawdaddy*, Nicks recalled how she stumbled into the relationship with Henley. It began with a telephone call from Henley while The Eagles and Fleetwood Mac were touring in different parts of the country. There followed a series of friendly and increasingly frequent phone calls from wherever the two bands happened to be, often miles apart. Finally Cupid stepped in and scheduled the two bands to play a series of concerts together.

"It was weird and fun," said Nicks. "The band arrived at the show and The Eagles were in the next dressing room. My attitude was that I would never just walk in there and say 'Hi. I'm Stevie'. I would rather die first.

So I go into our dressing room and there's this huge bouquet of roses with a card on it. I opened the card and it read 'The best of my love... Tonight? Don'. I thought that was about the uncoolest thing I'd ever seen in my whole life! I mean how could he possibly preconceive something like that? I was fuming and all of a sudden Christine (McVie) grabs me and takes me aside and says 'Don didn't send that, Mick (Fleetwood) and John (McVie) did.' They were in hysterics."

The practical joke quickly gave way to a formal introduction between Nicks and Henley. Friendship quickly blossomed into romance.

"It was during the 'One Of These Nights'/'Hotel California' period that I had my brief affair with Stevie Nicks," says Henley. "I remember The Eagles were on tour at the same time Fleetwood Mac was touring. One time I chartered a Lear jet and ran her to where I was and I got a lot of shit from the rest of the band about it. If she had a couple of days off, she'd come over and go on the road with us for a while and then I'd fly her back to wherever Fleetwood Mac was at. The affair with Stevie lasted off and on for about a year or so and we still remain good friends today."

Good friends maybe, but looking back on that affair for *GQ* in 1991, Henley dropped an unexpected footnote on his relationship with Nicks. "I believe, to the best of my knowledge, she became pregnant by me. And that she then had an abortion."

Another girlfriend of Henley's, Loree Rodkin, in the same *GQ* article, offered an interesting insight into the scene surrounding The Eagles and, in particular, Henley. "There was a dynamic of people making so much money at such a young age and wanting to do things like fly to Paris for dinner. That was the fast lane to me. I think, at the time, Don was more prone to having a girlfriend, whether that had parameters for him or not. Parameters like fidelity."

The Eagles returned from their shakedown dates with Walsh and finally decided it was time to enter the studio to make a follow-up to 'One Of These Nights'. Once again Bill Szymczyk was chosen to produce the album and he recalled being well aware of the pressure that hung over the band, and by association, himself. "Before 'One Of These Nights' The Eagles were a B-list band," he says. "With that album they were suddenly being considered an A-list band. People were suddenly beginning to think 'Oh these guys are real, they're going to be around for a while.' I think the expectancy was also exaggerated by the fact that Joe had joined the band."

They began recording what would become 'Hotel California' in March 1976 in The Record Plant in Los Angeles. But, recalled Meisner, "Bill was really worried about earthquakes and so we ended up moving to Criterion Studios in Florida and finishing it there."

The ever widening gap between Meisner and the rest of the band was reflected in where they chose to live during the sessions. "I rented this house on 461 Ocean Boulevard that was made famous by the Eric Clapton album. Everybody else stayed at the Coconut Grove."

The 'Hotel California' sessions were conspicuous, once again, by a lack of songs at the outset. March stretched into April and May without much being accomplished. Walsh, in a 1980 interview, revealed the complexities of those sessions and defended a recording process that would ultimately take eight months to complete. "It was taking a long time to get the album out because the attitude within the band was that we didn't want people to say here are some more Eagles' songs.

"We were these five guys in the studio and we all had some good ideas," he continued. "But nothing had really been written yet. It took a good three months of laying down tracks and rearranging them before we started to get the lyrics and hear the harmonies. We couldn't do it any faster and we didn't want to do it any faster."

The band was also distracted regularly on a number of fronts. Beginning on May 1, The Eagles introduced their newest member in grand fashion with a series of huge summer concerts that played havoc with their recording schedule. "Mixing those concerts up with our recording sessions was pure hell," reflected Meisner. "I remember one night we took a Lear jet from Miami to Houston, played the gig, flew back to Miami and worked on the album. There was a lot of stress."

Top: Left to right: Bernie Leadon, Don Henley, Randy Meisner, Glen Frey. (LFI)
Centre: Henley (right) and Leadon on stage in 1973. (Pictorial Press)
Bottom: Meisner, Henley, Frey and Leadon on stage. (Redferns)

Main picture, left to right: Leadon, Frey, Henley, Meisner and Don Felder. (Redferns)
Inset: (Redferns)

Top left: Joe Walsh (Retna); top right: Randy Meisner (Redferns); bottom left: Glen Frey (Pictorial); bottom right: Don Felder (Retna); centre: (Redferns).

Main picture: Joe Walsh at Wembley, June 1975. (retna); above, left to right:
Felder, Henley, Walsh and Leadon (all Pictorial Press).

Main picture: (Retna); top left, page 6: (Redferns), top right, page 6: (Retna); below, page 7: Elton John joins The Eagles on stage, April 1977 (Retna); inset, page 7: (Retna).

Top left: Joe Walsh (Redferns); top right: Timothy B. Schmit, on stage with The Eagles in 1979 (Retna); below: The last line-up of the Eagles on stage in Philadelphia, 1979.

Top left: Glen Frey (Retna); top right: Felder and Walsh (Redferns).

Main picture: Nils Lofgren jams with Joe Walsh (Retna);
inset: California Governor Jerry Brown and girlfriend Linda Rondstadt
on stage with The Eagles.

Top: Eagles manager Irving Azoff, second from right, backstage with the band; below: Henley in concert, 1979 (Retna).

On stage during the 1994 Hell Freezes Over reunion tour. Clockwise, from top left: Joe Walsh (Retna); Don Felder (Retna); Glen Frey, Joe Walsh and Don Felder (Redferns); Frey (Retna); Don Henley (Retna) and Schmit and Frey (Redferns).

Main picture: On stage during the Hell Freezes Over tour (Retna);
insets, left: (Pictorial Press); centre: (Redferns); right: (Pictorial Press).

Timothy B. Schmit (Taylor King)

Also, at a time when the band should have focused all their efforts on their own project, The Eagles were literally all over the map, playing on a number of new releases by their good buddies. Frey, Henley and Walsh appeared on J.D. Souther's second solo outing 'Black Rose'. Frey also played guitar on Carly Simon's 'Another Passenger', Walsh slung his axe on Rod Stewart's 'A Night On The Town' and Henley paid back Linda Ronstadt by singing on various tracks on her 'Hasten Down The Wind' album. Henley also appeared on Warren Zevon's 'Warren Zevon' and Jackson Browne's 'The Pretender'.

When they did find time to work on 'Hotel California', Meisner, whose marriage fell apart completely during the recording, found Frey and Henley's domination of the band to be quite overwhelming. "Don and Glenn were pretty much doing the album on their schedule instead of everybody else's," lamented Meisner, whose sole contribution to 'Hotel California' was the song 'Try And Love Again'. "It got to the point during the recording that the rest of the band was so tired that we just didn't care. Some days it would get to be four in the morning. We would have done a track 80 times and we'd all be looking at ourselves and saying 'Do you think that's a good one?'"

Producer Szymczyk, as diplomatically as possible, agreed with Meisner that Frey and Henley "were the chief nit pickers." "They would not leave something alone until they were a hundred percent satisfied with it. It could sometimes take two or three days to get a verse or a chorus or a guitar part to where they were satisfied with it. Then a week later we'd hit the record button and do it all over again."

Henley, however, claimed he and Frey "were just trying to get things right. We strived for perfection. We tried to get things in tune and tried to write lyrics that made sense. If that's perfectionism, I have no apologies to make for it."

Frey and Henley were no strangers to charges of dictatorial behaviour and were especially sensitive, in separate interviews over the years, to the claims that they ran roughshod over the 'Hotel California' sessions. "A band is supposed to be equal," said Frey, "but when people emerge as having certain strengths, other people are resentful of them having those strengths. Everybody makes this big deal about Don and I being the problem with the band. But I'm here to tell you right now that Joe Walsh and Don Felder and others created as much turbulence for the band as anybody else did."

Henley is equally adamant that trying to keep The Eagles a democracy was a real strain on Frey and himself. "We had a hard time keeping everybody happy. We spent a lot of time and energy just trying to keep the band together and trying to keep everybody happy and deal with everybody's emotional problems. I ended up getting an ulcer because of all the crap during 'Hotel California'.

"And it wasn't just what was going on in the band," he sighed, looking back on those sessions in 1991. "There was a lot of pressure from the record company, the fans, the managers, everybody. We needed a vacation and we didn't get one."

One night Meisner, after a particularly gruelling session, was unwinding in his ocean front home when there was a knock on the door. Standing in the dark, appearing slightly shadowy in the house lights, were Don Felder and Joe Walsh. Meisner could see the sleep lines and bloodshot eyes. They mirrored his own. He let them in.

"They were so mad at Don and Glenn," reflected Meisner of that night. "They said, 'They're just ruining everything and we don't like it'. I thought about what they were saying for a second and then I said 'Okay, you guys just want to start a trio?' They said that sounded like a great idea and we all agreed that night to do it when we finished the album and the next tour."

The recording, interspersed with big money live shows, continued through the summer and into Fall. Throughout the ordeal, Bill Szymczyk remained patient; prodding the band with subtle suggestions and encouragement and, from Frey, receiving the compliment that "Bill was very instrumental in helping us get our musical side down."

But, despite the progress, 'Hotel California' was fast becoming the talk of the music world. The group had missed so many deadlines for completing the album that The Eagles' record company had put the album on their 'indefinite release' list. Frey, with tongue firmly planted in cheek, addressed the question of the marathon pace of the 'Hotel California' sessions. "We don't do anything easy and maybe we make it harder than it has to be."

Henley, at another time and place, seemed to magically pick up on the thought. "I think this is a responsibility we have. If people are going to be opening their minds and hearts to us, we have to be saying something."

'Hotel California' was finally completed late in October and it arrived in the stores just in time for Christmas on December 8, 1976. What happened next was the best Christmas present The Eagles could have ever imagined.

Pushed along by a massive tide of favourable reviews, some by those who in the past had regularly dismissed the band, 'Hotel California' hit the top of the album charts on January 15, 1977 and held that position almost constantly for eight weeks. It ultimately stayed on the charts for 63 weeks. The first single from the album, 'New Kid In Town' hit No. 1 on February 26 and was certified gold on March 21. The follow up, 'Hotel California's' title track went to No. 1 on May 7 and was certified gold on May 12. A third single from the album, 'Life In The Fast Lane', reached No. 11 on June 25. The album was quickly certified platinum and, by 1995, had sold in excess of 12 million copies.

"When 'Hotel California' came out, we had no idea that it would be so big," a thoroughly shocked Walsh reflected in 1980. "We had worked on it for a year and it had gotten to the point where we hated it because we had worked on it for so long. It was all we heard for almost a year. When it came out and did so well it threw us. All of a sudden we were big."

But a stark list of chart statistics belies the true value of 'Hotel California'. Here was an album which finally brought The Eagles intellectual, as well as musical, kudos. Even their most ardent supporters were surprised by the deep, philosophical, ideas which the album promoted; a yearning for a California of a more innocent age when palm tress and orange groves spread out where urban tracts now littered the smog-engulfed landscape. But the hazy nostalgia was tempered with recrimination and a warning that too much excess brings with it a hollow, empty lifestyle – something of which The Eagles themselves were only too well aware. 'Hotel California' sought to pull the wraps off tinseltown, to expose it as a sad and lonely place where dreams too often turn to dust, to emphasise the truism that all that glitters is not gold. On another level altogether, it also finally fulfilled the band's hard rocking hopes as Joe Walsh's long, often heavy leads finally proclaimed The Eagles as a band with balls. These two factors are probably the reason why, especially in their own eyes, they could never seem to top this effort. For the best possible reasons, the Eagles shot their creative bolt with 'Hotel California'.

'Hotel California', with its recurring theme of idealism turning to disillusionment, effectively silenced those who had criticised the band's previous efforts as merely reflecting a laid-back California lifestyle. And, by association, it gave the members of the band much to talk about rather than a lot to defend themselves against.

"If you only listen to this album a few times it's going to sound like we're just singing about California," offered Frey. "But we're not. We're using California as a microcosm for the rest of the world. California is merely an example that everybody holds up to the light because California is simply the last frontier."

He suggested that the changing decade and the collective change in attitude were prime influences in the thoughtful, philosophical lyrics that rage on the album's songs. "We've been thinking a lot about the apathetic, watchful Seventies. It seems like love and revolution were all exploited in the Seventies and we all came up empty handed. We need heroes right now, and this album is trying to tell people that the individual is the next big thing, and that the future will depend on how you live your life."

Henley echoed the notion of 'Hotel California' as a vinyl metaphor for a kind of spiritual reawakening. "The new album is about trying to look at things a different way. To go on from here and try to develop a new set of values and a new thrill that's more meaningful and more valid then one just built on sand. It's a lot like this band. Some of the first thrills had had no real roots, no base or anything. But the intentions we had were good.

"It's kind of about the demise of the Sixties and the decadence and escapism we're experiencing in the Seventies. This album is an attempt to shake people out of the apathy they're going through."

It was also an attempt to show the world that The Eagles had grown up. "The songs we wrote and sang when we were 23, 24, 25 had a certain optimism and naïveté about them," explained Henley. "I think, as we grew more experienced and more confident, we felt that, maybe, we could write about other things."

Henley picked up on that train of thought in the mid-Eighties *Musician* interview. "I agree with some of the critics now that a lot of the early Eagles' songs were the result of our being young, immature and male chauvinists. But a lot of those early songs were collaborative efforts and not necessarily my opinions. Just to get a song written is hard enough. Sometimes you don't quite have the time to sit down and reflect on whether you're being objective or you're being fair or right or not. It's just emotion and so sometimes it just gushes out.

"The one thing that's been constant about all the songs and all the records is that we tried to tell the truth, no matter how large or small the vision was. So the fact that things have suddenly gotten darker meant one thing to me. We were growing up, getting older and finding out that power and money didn't solve problems but just changed the face of them."

Henley picked up the defence of The Eagles later that year when, in tones as close to angry as he ever gets, he told *Crawdaddy* that he had it up to here with the band's songs being dismissed as AM radio pap. "I do think the songs are underrated," he groused. "Our songs just don't get enough attention. That's the fast lane for us, working on the songs. People talk about Jackson's (Browne) lyrics but they don't seem to talk about ours. It's not that they don't look at us as good songwriters but they just seem to emphasise the songs that were hits rather than the ones that weren't. They don't seem to think you can write a catchy tune that's a hit that means something. I think our songs have more to do with the streets than Bruce Springsteen's."

The Eagles had no time to sit around and toast their success. On March 14, 1977 the group embarked on a month long tour of the US, then crossed the Atlantic for a month long tour of Europe followed by dates in Japan and Australia. They returned in May, just in time to hitch a ride on another round of outdoor stadium shows. The 1977 tours offered pretty much a carbon copy of the previous year's set list. The more rocking elements of 'Hotel California', featuring much improved guitar interplay between Walsh and Felder, made for some fiery moments before the band settled into the comparative safety of softies like 'One Of These Nights', 'New Kid In Town' and 'Wasted Time'.

During the outdoor concerts in May the band hit trouble. "We started getting pushed along by the momentum rather than controlling it," explained Henley. Nerves were frayed. Arguments that used to start off good natured quickly escalated into real anger.

Walsh remembered the scene on the road at that time as being "paranoid and crazy". Henley reflected on one night in particular when it all came to a head in a hotel somewhere in the great American heartland. "We had just had this big blowout. I don't remember how it started and who it involved. But I do remember that it ended up with all of us just sitting in a room and talking things out. What basically came out of it was that 'Hey, we sure have accomplished a lot. We've given it 11 months, we're a little bit tired and sometimes we tend to get a little bit crazy but we understand what's happening and can deal with it."

That worked for the moment but Meisner, with no small discomfort, remembered that "the stress was still there. And it was getting worse." He recalled the night his own personal stress reached critical mass, following a typical third encore at a concert in Knoxville, Tennessee. "We had just come offstage and I was beat, stressed out and I had the flu and I was just plain grumpy. We had done our third encore and I was ready to pack it in for the night when, all of a sudden, the band decides to go out again. I said 'God! we've already done three encores and I don't feel well.' Glenn got right up in my face and called me a pussy and I just snapped and took a swing at him. There were police backstage and they grabbed me. Glenn grabbed up a towel, wiped his sweaty face on it and just threw it in my face.

"I said 'That's it'. "I quit the band for all intents and purposes that night. But I went ahead and finished the rest of the US tour and that second trip back to Europe. My last days as an Eagle were pure hell. Nobody was talking to me."

The final insult for Meisner occurred when the band returned to the States. He approached Felder and Walsh about their previous agreement to leave The Eagles and form a new band. "They had totally backed out of it," said a still bitter Meisner. "Their attitude was that they couldn't care less about my situation. Up to that point, I had always thought of them as my friends. Since that time I've always thought of them as traitors."

Chapter VIII

The Long Run

Timothy B. Schmit, born November 20, 1947 in Sacramento, California, learned music from the best. His dad. His earliest childhood memories are of sitting aboard a trailer, rumbling up and down the picturesque Californian coast. By day his father would sell vacuum cleaners. By night he would play violin and stand up bass in any small club with a gig to offer. Finally, when young Timothy B. reached school age, the Schmit family settled in Sacramento where the elder Schmit gave up the vacuum cleaner business in favour of a full time gig as the house musician.

Schmit's early musical training pretty much reflected the tenor of the times. When folk was popular in the early Sixties, Schmit, in 1963, formed one half of a folk duo called Tim and Ron. In 1962, when everybody was riding the surf craze with The Beach Boys, the duo added a guitarist and became a surf trio called The Contenders.

The Contenders were barely wet behind the ears when, in 1964, the arrival of The Beatles inspired Schmit and his friends to adopt mop tops and emerge as a very British influenced New Breed who were favourites on the local club and dance circuit.

"My father was so proud that I was following in his footsteps," remembered Schmit when he was singing and playing bass for the New Breed. "I remember one night, before a local show, I was all dressed up like a Beatle and he could see that I was really going for it. He was real proud. He was a real happy man."

When not fronting The New Breed, Schmit attended Sacramento State College where he majored in psychology. Changing their name to Glad in the mid-Sixties, his band's reputation was beginning to reach beyond the Sacramento city limits and, in 1968, they were signed to ABC Records. About that time Richie Furay was in the process of putting together Poco and he invited Schmit to try out with them.

Feeling guilty about abandoning his high school chums, Schmit went to a couple of auditions, but was not too disappointed when he lost out to another bassist, Randy Meisner, who could sing the high notes. Schmit continued with Glad and stayed at college but he kept a wary eye open to the fortunes of Poco too. When Meisner quit on the eve of Poco's first album, 'Picking Up The Pieces', being released midway through 1969 , Schmit played a few test shows while still continuing with Glad. He dropped out of college 18 units short of a degree.

Glad released one eponymous album in January 1970 which went nowhere. The band, now a full time occupation, was having money problems, so in February 1970, Schmit made what he conceded "to be a really tough decision", and left Glad to join Poco.

Timothy Schmit remained with Poco for seven years, watching in frustration as they continued to ride the wave of critical opinion but rarely saw the inside of the Top Forty. "It was frustrating," Schmit once reflected. "We were a good band with good musicians but it just couldn't seem to happen for us."Ironically, it would be two years after Schmit left the band that Poco would finally land its first gold record for the album 'Legend'.

In 1977, Schmit received a call from Glenn Frey, whose long memory recalled the nights that Poco shared the stage with Longbranch Pennywhistle. He wanted to know if he was interested in replacing Randy Meisner a second time, only this time as an Eagle. He jumped at the chance. "I feel real blessed," said Schmit of the offer in 1979. "I've never done anything but what I love to do to make money and now I could become very wealthy soon."

Rather than rest on their laurels as 'Hotel California' continued to sell in massive quantities, The Eagles, and Frey and Henley in particular, were already thinking seriously about their next album when Schmit joined the flock.

"Music is a lot of hard work," Frey once said in response to the impression of The Eagles as a bunch of workaholics. "This is not something you leave at the office. This is something I take around with me all the time... every minute I'm awake, and even when I'm asleep. I'm worried about the next album, what's going to be written about it and how we're going to make it better than the last one."

Looking back on those post 'Hotel California' days in 1989, Henley questioned the wisdom of rushing into another album so soon. "We needed a vacation," he said. "We needed to take some time off and away from each other and we didn't do it. Because there was that pressure from the record company and ourselves to follow up 'Hotel California' with another one of those.

"Instead of taking a year off after 'Hotel California' to sit back, take a deep breath and assess the situation and figure out what direction we should go in, we plunged right into another album. We were pretty much paralysed. I didn't have much left to say at that point. I don't think any of us did. We were pretty tired."

Joe Smith, chairman of the board of Elektra/Asylum Records, was acutely aware of the importance of a new Eagles' album to the company's bottom line at that time. "Renegotiating The Eagles' contract was an ongoing thing," he says. "Every time they would release an album, Irving (Azoff) would come in and renegotiate. It was nothing for them to really exert some economic impact on the label. The Eagles holding back a record might represent $35 million, $40 million in lost revenue."

Irving Azoff was acutely aware of this and used the situation to his, and The Eagles' maximum advantage. Most managers of multi-platinum bands do the same thing – force a renegotiation, effectively a royalty hike, under the implied threat that without one there might be a delay in the delivery of his clients' next album. Azoff said in 1979 that renegotiating The Eagles' contract was in line with his motto of "Pay now, pay more later. I would figure out a fair price, add a third and that's what we get in our contracts."

But Azoff also knew better than to rush a band of scrupulous perfectionists like The Eagles, so Smith could be seen visibly twisting in the wind throughout much of 1977 as individual members yet again made themselves quite visible on records by others. Don Henley drummed and sang on Linda Ronstadt's 'Simple Dreams', Glenn Frey sang on the début Columbia LP by Karla Bonoff, and on Joni Mitchell's

'Don Juan's Reckless Daughter'. Frey, Henley, Schmit and Walsh appeared on the Randy Newman album 'Little Criminals', while Henley and Schmit also found the time to make an appearance on the début LP of cult singer-songwriter Terence Boylan.

When the band eventually began making tentative plans for a follow up to 'Hotel California', producer Bill Szymczyk referred to it as "the impossible dream." "In reality," Szymczyk told *Billboard* early in 1978, "we felt more pressure doing 'One Of These Nights'. I don't think we feel any special pressure on this next album."

Szymczyk predicted that the album, with a working title of 'What Would Robert Mitchum Do?', would feature... "a more hard rock sound. There will be at least one country flavoured story-telling ballad because the band does them so well. But overall I think you'll be hearing more stuff like 'Life In The Fast Lane'. The LP will be straight ahead American rock and roll."

In January 1978 the song 'Hotel California' was nominated by the Grammy committee for Record Of The Year. The Eagles were invited to perform on the Grammy Awards Show, scheduled for February 28, but true to their rugged individualist ways, they not only declined to perform but didn't even turn up when 'Hotel California' did indeed pick up a Grammy for Record Of The Year. Like just about every tale surrounding this band, the truth of what went on behind the scenes depends on who you wish to believe.

According to the show's producer, Pierre Cossette, as reported in *Rolling Stone* and the book *Broken Record: The Inside Story Of The Grammy Awards*, Irving Azoff agreed to have the band appear on the show only if Cossette could guarantee that they would win an award. When the producer said there was no way winners would be known in advance, Azoff reportedly countered with the suggestion that the band be provided with a secret dressing room and that they would come out if they won. Naturally, Azoff denied the producer's charges.

Frey later stated that the reason why the band snubbed the Grammys was because they were in Malibu working on songs for the next album.

"We had work to do and the new record was more important than showing up and resting on past laurels," he said. With tongue firmly planted in cheek, Frey also took the opportunity to take a poke at awards shows in general and the Grammys in particular. "There's a credibility gap. Debby Boone wins Best New Artist and Warren Zevon and Karla Bonoff don't even get nominated. I have reasonable doubt about how accurately any kind of contest or award show can portray the year in music."

Frey's explanation for The Eagles' absence would appear to be closer to the truth for, on March 9, 1978, The Eagles stepped into the One Step Up recording studio in Los Angeles and laid down the initial tracks for the song 'I Can't Tell You Why', the first small, concrete step forward on the next album. Adding further weight to the stone they were pushing was the fact that the band, in the name of democracy, decided that 'The Long Run' should be a double album. "We decided we would do a double album," said Frey, "so that way no one worries 'Is this the only song I'm going to get to do?'"

Distractions were continually thrown in the way of the album's progress, not least a long simmering feud with the editorial staff of *Rolling Stone* magazine which was to be settled on a baseball diamond. If The Eagles had lost the softball tussle they would have had to submit to an interview with a magazine that had consistently dismissed the band. Fortunately for them the final score was Eagles 15 – *Rolling Stone* 8.

As ever the group continued to pop up on every conceivable session. Felder and Frey appeared on the Bob Seger album 'Stranger In Town', and members of the band appeared on J.D. Souther's 'You're Only Lonely' and Karla Bonoff's 'Restless Nights'. Joe Walsh managed to find the time to release another solo LP entitled 'But Seriously Folks' which featured contributions from the band. The Walsh song 'Life's Been Good' and The Eagles' 'Life In The Fast Lane' ended up on the soundtrack for the movie *FM*, of which Irving Azoff was an original executive producer. Steely Dan, also clients of Azoff, wrote and performed the title track with various Eagles on backing vocals, but somewhere along the line Azoff's name was removed from the credits at his own request, a wise decision in view of the critical bashing it subsequently received.

In July the 'Long Run' sessions, now relocated to the Bayshore Recording Studio in Coconut Grove, Florida, were put on hold while the band undertook a month long Canadian tour. When they got back to the studio in August 1978, there was a pile of messages, most of them from their record company. "We only hear from them about 10 times a month," chuckled Azoff during the recording of 'The Long Run'. "When they project a $116 million year because Linda Ronstadt and The Eagles are releasing albums and then come up $40 million short because they don't get an Eagles album, well then they hurt. But you just can't rush this band. It has to be done at their own speed."

Despite the coaxing of producer Bill Szymczyk, the 'Long Run' sessions were moving at the proverbial snail's pace. Eventually they would turn into the kind of marathon endurance test that is all too frequent among platinum acts of the Nineties, but back in 1978, the length of the session became the talk of the industry, and a byword for gratuitous studio indulgence. Perhaps someone should have reminded The Eagles that The Beatles' first album, still widely regarded as a landmark in rock, was recorded in just one day.

One night Henley showed off his near manic penchant for perfection by tinkering for over five hours with the rhythm track of the song 'Heartache Tonight', sequencing in thumps from a big bass drum to give the song the desired kick. Frey wandered in and out of the control room, occasionally exchanging a joke or a suggestion with Henley but, to a large extent, staying out of the way. Walsh, who showed up thinking he was going to get the opportunity to lay down some lead riffs, saw he wouldn't get the chance and eventually left. Finally, as the clock struck midnight, Henley and Frey emerged from the control room, left the studio and went down to a local dive for a drink.

Szymczyk would later remark that the record took so long to come together that they gave it the nickname of 'The Long One'. He was often hard pressed to figure out why it was taking so long. "But some of what was going on during those sessions was really unavoidable," he reflected. "For example, Glenn and Don would bring in the chord changes and rhythm of a song without having done the lyrics. When you cut a track and don't have any idea what the song's about, it's difficult to take an attitude about the tune. So a musician naturally tends to treat it standoffishly. With The Eagles, a lot of times a track was recorded before it was completely written in the hopes that the rest of the band would give feedback and help develop it. And that ended up taking time."

Azoff was concerned about the physical and emotional strain that recording 'The Long Run' was putting on the band. But he was confident what the results would be. "I knew they were incapable of putting less than three No. 1 records on the album. When Henley and Frey sit down to write a song, the hits just come out. Them writing songs is like you and me drinking water."

Elektra-Asylum became increasingly worried as the sessions continued through the fall of 1978. Joe Smith and his accountants were literally pleading for Eagles product, any Eagles product. More to placate their company than anything else, The Eagles knocked out a seasonal single, a remake of the Charles Brown song 'Please Come Home For Christmas' backed with their original 'Funky New Year'. The record company was not overwhelmed but they accepted the single and released it on December 23. It went to No. 18 on the *Billboard* charts.

The New Year came and went with The Eagles continuing their long and deliberate assault on 'The Long Run'. By now they had decided that a double album was out of the question and so, with new songs still being written, they started to whittle down the projected 18 songs to a more manageable single disc. This was a decision which ruffled a few more feathers on the already ruffled plume of Don Felder. "I've written 15 to 25 songs for each Eagles record and out of those we'd end up selecting maybe two that represented The Eagles' style," he said.

"In any given week, I'll write a couple of songs. I've given all my time over to writing songs for The Eagles. But right now I have an over abundance of songs that just don't seem to fit."

Their other guitarist, happy-go-lucky Joe Walsh, could usually be counted on to put the best possible spin on the most negative situation, and was surprisingly candid in assessing the collective disarray within the band at the time. "The atmosphere in the band at the time was paranoid. The group just lost its perspective. We just kind of sat around in a daze for months. The tapes were running but nobody knew what was going on."

And so the session for 'The Long Run' continued at a tortoise like pace, stretching beyond a year towards 18 months. "I tend to be meticulous but, for that album, I considered that I was working fast and that the band was working slow," said Szymczyk. "Fortunately the band decided to cut it down to a single album. We had been working on it for 18 months and we still hadn't finished it. If it had been a double album, we might still be working on it today."

Henley was depressed to realise that some of the problems they thought they had eradicated with the departure of Leadon and Meisner were reappearing. "Things were okay for a while and then there was another uprising," he sighed. "The group once again split up into factions. In the end, even Glenn and I were not necessarily on the same side of the fence; although that was not primarily because of a rift between Glenn and myself. There were rifts all over the place and between all kinds of people. It was great for a minute and then the same old demons reared their ugly heads."

The record company was getting desperate; so desperate, in fact, that *Fortune* magazine reported in an early 1979 issue that Elektra-Asylum had offered the band a $1 million bonus if they have the album ready for release that summer. It came as no surprise to Joe Smith when the band missed the deadline too. "You're dealing with people who have so much money that there is no financial spur," lamented Smith in *Fortune*. "We even sent them a rhyming dictionary."

Late Summer 1979. The Eagles seem to be finally buckling down to the reality of getting 'The Long Run' completed more than 15 months after beginning the project. On a typical night in the studio, producer Szymczyk is behind the board. Henley is jotting down some last minute structural changes. Junk food wrappers, soda and beer cans clutter the studio. The occasional beer can dots the floor and control board. As the night gets older and turns into morning, it is possible to get a contact high off the marijuana smoke settling in the air. Henley is burning on a short fuse but he still had his sense of humour.

"My ulcer is acting up," chuckled Henley when a friendly *Rolling Stone* correspondent dropped by the studio. "But that's a good sign. Its last appearance was at the beginning of 'Hotel California'. I estimate we're about sixty percent done with this album."

Henley's health was a major consideration in 'The Long Run' sessions. "We did have to inch our way along for a while but, once we got going, it was easier than 'Hotel California'. One reason was that I took better care of myself. I tried to stay healthy and not take as many drugs. Frankly, when we started this album, I was worried that I might get sick if we pushed ourselves as hard as we had done with 'Hotel California'. Physically and mentally I don't think we could have taken it."

Schmit, who with Poco had become used to the idea of turning out a new album every six months, admitted that it took some mental readjustment to slow himself down to the pace of The Eagles during 'The Long Run' sessions but he managed to put the problem in its proper perspective. "I was surprised at the thoroughness of The Eagles' recording process," he admitted. "From where I stood no element of the music was being overlooked."

In *The Los Angeles Times* Walsh described the moment when the band broke through the invisible wall separating them from the creative spurt to the finishing line. "It started to come together when we were doing the song 'Heartache Tonight'," remembered the guitarist. "Glenn went out and sung his ass off on that track. We knew at that point that we were off the hook a little. We knew at that point that we had a single. The next break on that album came when we recorded 'The Long Run'. When Henley sang those words, we knew we had the beginning of a concept. The next step was 'Sad Café'. Once again it was in the words. That's when we were finally able to say to ourselves 'Hey! This is going to be okay.'"

"You can never predict how much an album will sell or how critics will react to you," he continued. "The only thing you can ask yourself is whether you feel you are making a valid statement. That's the only measure you can realistically apply. After 'Sad Café' we felt the answer was yes."

Mid-August. Henley calls up a few close friends and acquaintances to announce that 'The Long Run'... "will definitely be finished in a couple of days." A week later, no album. And those who flew in for the occasion are treated to the disconcerting spectre of Henley and Szymczyk still trying to nail down the last few words to the song 'Disco Strangler' while roadies and hangers on wander the studio, with dazed expressions and flying saucer eyes.

Henley is an agonising picture of too much indulgence and too little sleep as he sits crouched in a corner of the studio. Struggling to get the right words that will end it all. "Let's finish this sonovabitch so I can go home and throw up some more," he spat.

Frey, doing his best to maintain some semblance of decorum, washed down some vitamins with a gulp of soda and then, according to eye witness reports, lost it. "I hate this song! I hate this album! God help me! I'm bumming!"

Schmit, a picture of calm even in his most dishevelled moments, cracked a distasteful joke about Henley and the control board performing an indecent act together.

The last minute fine tuning of the last song goes on and on and on. Those who had arrived hours earlier, hoping for the long anticipated first listen, begin to sense it was not going to happen and drifted off into the night.

Three a.m.. Henley and manager Irving Azoff exchange opinions.

"I'm tired and I'm rich and I can do what I want," said Azoff. "I'm going home to sleep."

"If I can stay up, you can stay up," retorted Henley.

"Yeah," slurred Azoff, "but you're tougher than I am."

Henley had the last word. "You can stay up."

And so Azoff stayed up.

September 1, 1979. 5:46 a.m. 'The Long Run', The Eagles' last studio album, is completed. "It's over. We made it and it ate us," murmured Szymczyk, emerging battered and beat like a prisoner released after 20 years inside.

'The Long Run' was released on September 22, 1979, and made an immediate impact on the charts. The song 'I Can't Tell You Why' reached No. 8 as did the title track. The song 'Heartache Tonight' turned out to be the album's biggest hit, reaching No. 1 in November and certified gold in February 1980. The album went to No. 1 in November and remained at the top for nine weeks, ultimately selling more than five million copies.

In retrospect, this album – dredged out during what was probably the lowest point in the band's career – has no business being as good as it is. 'The Long Run' is a low key affair for the most part, sprinkled liberally with a more self-effacing sense of humour than on previous Eagles' releases. Had this album not been three years in the making and been obliged to follow 'Hotel California', it might have been received more favourably. As it is 'The Long Run' found The Eagles running frantically inwards, away from the very things that were consuming them. But somewhere inside they found quiet solace in the things that always mattered most to them: quality, melody and an almost painful degree of perfection.

Critics who praised 'Hotel California' reverted to form in dismissing 'The Long Run' as a poor follow-up. The acerbic Dave Marsh even went so far as to claim that the band's song 'The Long Run' was actually a thinly disguised rip-off of the Otis Clay song, 'Trying To Live My Life Without You'. The jury is still out on that charge but the mixed reviews were even reflected by its two main architects, Frey and Henley.

"I think 'The Long Run' is a bit underrated. But you can also hear that it is slightly tired," Frey said not long after it was released. In a later assessment, he said: "I think the big lesson we learned with 'The Long Run' is that you have to strive for perfection but, in rock and roll, you have to settle for excellence. We tried for three and a half years to make 'The Long Run' perfect and we couldn't."

Henley was initially philosophical about what the album meant to the band. "I think this lets people know that we're persistent if nothing else. We're kind of proud for lasting this long. Also people have often said that our songs are cynical and bummers. I think the songs on this album are pretty positive."

In hindsight, he was less charitable. "We probably should have just given up, written a couple of more love songs and put 'The Long Run' out a couple of years earlier," he said, adding, in a masterly understatement: "We spent too much time working on that album." He continued to denigrate the album in a 1989 *Musician* interview. "I don't think it's a very good album at all and it depresses me to listen to it. We were so miserable making that album that it actually got funny at one point. Our humour actually got very dark and very sick and that's in the songs 'Teenage Jail' and 'The Greeks Don't Want No Freaks'. But by and large I don't think that's a very good record. We didn't have a good time making it. We were sick and tired of each other."

But the band were on an up when they hit the road in the wake of 'The Long Run' for yet another tour of the States. The shows were a series of scintillating exercises in stage perfection with the band very much in synch, and the reviews were among the best The Eagles ever received.

The band opened with 'Hotel California' and played the snappier tunes from the new album – 'The Long Run', 'Heartache Tonight' and 'I Can't Tell You Why', before easing down on the accelerator for the soft-centered tunes from early in their career. Audiences at every stop on the tour reacted almost hysterically to the shows, a source of some amusement to Henley who, in the comfort of his hotel suite after one show, reflected on that aspect with *LA Times* rock critic Robert Hilburn.

"It's funny because I thought that things might slack off a bit on this tour. But the crowds have been going nuts. There seems to be an increased bond between the audience and the band. I don't know why exactly. Maybe it's just that we've been around a long time. Maybe it's just that we've all survived."

The group, to a large extent press shy during the 'Hotel California' period, became more candid in discussing what they had endured during the recent 'Long Run' sessions and what this meant for the future of The Eagles. "We've always had this laid-back image that I think is a holdover from our early days as a band," Felder told the *LA Times*. "But that was nine years ago and those feelings are long gone. Everybody is satisfied with what's happening with this band but, at the same time, the effort required to maintain ourselves in this position isn't what you would call a peaceful, easy feeling."

Manager Azoff, who during this tour was often spotted jumping up and down enthusiastically as the band played, described the 'Long Run' sessions in tones that suggested it had been a trial by fire. "The recording of 'The Long Run' could have broken them," he said. "The longer you're in a band, if you let your standards slip, the harder it is. But I think the reaction to this album has convinced the band that it can face up to whatever pressures come their way. The feeling in the band is probably better than it has ever been."

But Azoff did sound a cautionary note. "The thing that keeps them together is that they enjoy the music. If that music doesn't continue to hold them, it could all disintegrate in a second."

At the end of a long day after a particularly successful show in Miami, Henley, who often seemed to find the downside to everything, was surprisingly hopeful. "I never thought we'd get this far. It looked for a while like we were going to break up every year until the people who were threatening to leave the band did leave. To tell the truth I am getting tired. Sometimes I feel like quitting one day and then I feel like going on forever the next day.

"Personally I think we can sustain this level for at least one or two more albums; at least a concert album and a studio album. What I think I'd like to do is make a really great studio album, maybe even a double album, to go out on. I'd like to go out gracefully rather than wait until it starts going down."

Chapter IX

Breaking Up Is Easy To Do

Glenn Frey is probably the last person most people would expect to put a positive spin on The Eagles' long-standing internal problems. But in 1977, when the rigours of 'Hotel California' were threatening to destroy the band, he was insistent that they would survive. "I think the key to our longevity is that this is a group of people who hang together no matter what, it would be very easy to break up. It's very inspiring. It gets me off that we've been together this long and have had the problems we've had and still know that we're better off together. In my most outrageous moment I'm not going to wreck this."

But, by the time the dust settled on 'The Long Run', Frey was singing a different tune. "The band was like a fake democracy. Henley and I were making the decisions while, at the same time, trying to pacify, include and cajole the others. There was always so much turbulence around our band that it made us serious all the time. There never was a day when all five guys felt good."

While 'The Long Run' enjoyed a reasonably long run on the charts, the individual members of The Eagles took yet another busman's holiday to appear on a batch of albums by others. Don Henley added his vocals to the début LP by Christopher Cross. Henley, Frey, Felder and Walsh contributed to the Warren Zevon album 'Bad Luck Streak In A Dancing School'. Walsh, for his part, took the time out from a goofy run at the presidency to play guitar on Graham Nash's 'Earth And Sky' while Henley, Frey and Schmit added their support to Bob Seger's 'Against The Wind'.

It was also at this point that the band, particularly Frey and Henley, began getting involved in social and political causes. Frey jokingly suggested they started doing benefits "because Linda Ronstadt started going out with (then California Governor) Jerry Brown." But in a 1990 *Rolling Stone* interview, Henley reflected on how that road was paved with potholes.

"We learned that it was not really a good idea to do benefit concerts for individual politicians. We got a lot of flak for that. At first we did a lot of benefits for Indian tribes in California. And then Jackson Browne kind of influenced us to get involved in the anti-nuclear movement and some more political things. But we always had to be careful. Politics is a dirty game and being involved on any level could have hurt us or the people or movement we were trying to support."

On February 27, 1980, The Eagles made their second trip to the Grammys and won the Best Rock Vocal Performance by a duo or group for the song 'Heartache Tonight'. In May the group, collectively and with others, landed two slots on the soundtrack to the movie *Urban Cowboy*. Walsh went solo on the song 'All Night Long' while the entire band, joined by Bob Seger, offered up a fresh rendition of 'Lyin' Eyes'.

But despite their continued visibility and massive success, this was a band that was spiritually and emotionally on its last legs. "In some ways the success took a lot of fun out of it," said Frey. "Putting pressure on ourselves also took a lot of fun out of it. I think Henley took some of the fun out of it for me and I'm sure I took some of the fun out of it for him. Unfortunately, what happens when you really make it is that you begin to look at your career in terms of how much each album sold."

In a *GQ* interview in 1991, when his solo career was cooking, Henley acknowledged that The Eagles' problems had been building and festering since 1977. "A lot of the tension surrounding the making of 'The Long Run' was because Glenn and Felder were at odds," he said. "But finally we just got tired. It was as simple as that. We got tired. We ran out of inspiration and to follow 'Hotel California' was such a monumental task, it just scared us. Due to fatigue, nervousness and craziness, some verbal exchanges went down during the making of 'The Long Run' that didn't heal. We used to just get in a room and fight it out and talk it out. But it got to a point after a while that we stopped communicating and that's death."

Henley suggested also that the death of The Eagles could be attributed to the fact that he and Frey wanted to go their separate creative ways. "Right after 'Hotel California' is when Glenn and I started growing in opposite directions. I wanted to write about all these social issues and he didn't. So we just grew apart musically and philosophically."

Unofficially The Eagles broke up after that stormy benefit concert in Long Beach. After the dust had settled on the backstage blow-up and cooler heads prevailed, Frey called Henley on the phone to tell him he would be working on a solo project. Henley read between the lines and knew it was over.

"He didn't say that he was through with the group but I knew what he meant," says Henley. "He was tired of all the diplomacy and compromise necessitated by a group situation. Still, I was shocked and hurt. You just don't think of ending something that was great."

Henley knew The Eagles were dead and buried with Frey's telephone call. "We broke up in 1980," Henley said in a *GQ* interview, "and nobody really knew about it until 1982 because the managers and the record company didn't want to tell anybody. They thought 'Oh they'll get over it'.

"I can only describe it as sort of a horrible relief," he added. "I was shocked and hurt. It was the beginning of what turned out to be a terrible year."

For Henley, the year reached rock bottom when Los Angeles police arrived at his home and discovered a naked 16-year-old girl suffering from a drug overdose. Henley was arrested and charged with possession of marijuana, cocaine and Quaaludes, and contributing to the delinquency of a minor. He was fined, put on two years' probation and ordered to attend drug counselling. For a number of years Henley refused to discuss the particulars of the arrest. But he acknowledged the situation for *GQ* in 1991. He claimed that the Fire Department was the first on the scene and that they "flat out lied to me."

"They said 'Well by law we're supposed to take this little girl to the hospital but, if you'll take care of her, we'll leave her here.' They said they were not here to get anybody busted. She was fine by the time they got there. I had no idea how old she was and I had no idea she was doing that many drugs. I didn't have sex with her. Yes, she was a hooker. Yes, I called a Madame. Yes, there were roadies and guys at my house. We were having a farewell to The Eagles.

"I got all of them out of the house and I took complete blame for everything. I was stupid. I could have flushed everything down the toilet. I didn't want this girl dying in my house. I wanted to get her medical attention. I did what I thought was best and I paid the price. At that point I thought it was probably the end of my career."

The slow but steady decline of the band as a profit making machine was not lost on Elektra-Asylum Records and chairman Joe Smith. Smith spent half of 1979 and half of 1980 trying to convince the band to do a live album.

"Everybody could see that they were having problems internally and that this was probably going to be their last hurrah," he says. "Finally they agreed to do the live album but they did so very reluctantly. Henley and Frey were getting further and further apart personally and the thought of having to spend time in an editing room together or to even come up with a new song or two scared them to death."

The Eagles agreed to do a series of concerts at the Long Beach Arena and Santa Monica Civic in Southern California in July 1980 to be recorded for a double live LP. Everything seemed in order when, the night before the first show, Smith received a telephone call from Irving Azoff.

"He tells me we have a problem," Smith recalls. "The problem means I'm not getting the album. Then Irving said the guys want to get on the phone and tell you themselves. So Don and Glenn get on and say 'Look, we really don't want to do this. We really don't want to spend that much time with each other. We could do a short tour and not record and be finished. But we promised you we'd do this so we're giving you a chance if you can answer one question.'"

Smith responded. "What's the question?"

"In 1971 the Baltimore Orioles had four 20 game winners. If you can name them, we'll do the album."

Smith thought for a moment. He was a baseball fan but he was drawing a blank. Finally, after what seemed like forever, it came to him. "I said Dave McNally, Jim Palmer, Mike Cuellar and Pat Dobson."

There was a pause at the other end of the line. Finally Frey came back with "Okay, we'll do the album and we'll see you tomorrow."

Smith could not believe his luck. "I asked them what they would have done if I had not answered the question correctly? Their response was 'We'd go on tour and you'd never have that live album.' And I could tell that they weren't kidding."

The concerts went off without a hitch. But when the band and producer Szymczyk returned to the familiar confines of Florida to mix the tapes, the breach between Frey and Henley had reached such proportions that Frey remained in Los Angeles and refused to join them. Things became so tense, in fact, that when The Eagles' record company offered them an extra $2 million advance if two new songs appeared on the album, they turned it down.

Logistically 'Eagles Live' was a nightmare, with tapes having to be flown back and forth between the studios in Miami and Los Angeles where Frey would listen and judge the music. Nevertheless, Szymczyk recalls that 'Live' was probably the easiest Eagles' album to record.

"We knocked the 'Eagles Live' album out in a month. The big difference was that everybody knew the songs in front and we didn't have to wait two months for somebody to write words for the last chorus of a particular song. Everybody knew the material and so it was just a matter of putting it down perfectly in technical terms. I had my assistant with Glenn in Los Angeles and I had the rest of the band in Miami. We were fixing three-part harmonies by Federal Express."

Indeed, the harmonies were so perfect that when 'Eagles Live' was released on November 7, 1980, the press suggested that it was actually a collection of studio sessions with the audience response overdubbed. Producer Szymczyk defended the band:

"We did patch the tracks up here and there, but everybody does that with a live album. The band does sound like their albums in concert and I'd say that 70 percent of the record is live. Not that it's easy to record a singing drummer like Don, because you have to make sure your vocal mike is aimed in a particular way to prevent a lot of sound leakage.

That should prove that all of Henley's vocals are live... because it would be almost impossible to overdub, keeping the drum track and putting on a different vocal."

'Eagles Live' reached No. 6 on the album charts and, to date, has sold in excess of two million copies. It also generated The Eagles' very last chart single, their cover of Steve Young's 'Seven Bridges Road', which reached No. 27.

For what turned out to be the band's last hurrah, 'Eagles Live' is no better or worse than any number of similar live albums. The temptation is to listen between the lines, to try and sense a hint of the tension that was tearing the band apart as the harmonies flowed on, but there is nothing – not a trace – and this in itself is a remarkable achievement. Whatever ailed them, whatever tensions pulled at the strings which still somehow held them together, The Eagles always called a truce when they hit the stage.

Although The Eagles' flight was essentially over, no announcement was forthcoming throughout 1981. Henley, Frey and Walsh were all busy on solo projects and, once again, the individuals were conspicuous on the session front. Schmit sang on Gary Wright's 'The Right Place' and on Joe Vitale's 'Plantation Harbor'. Walsh and Felder played on Joe Vitale's album. Henley again teamed up with Stevie Nicks, this time professionally, playing guitar, singing background vocals and drumming and singing duets with Nicks on her début solo album 'Bella Donna'. Walsh, as summer turned to fall, turned up on Who bassist John Entwistle's 'Too Late The Hero', Schmit sang on Quarterflash's début LP and Felder played guitar on The Bee Gees 'Living Eyes'.

On the topic of The Eagles, however, the band, eternally shy of interviews, had little to say. The most telling comment, one that seemed to reflect the bitterness, came in 1982, shortly before the official announcement of the break-up when Frey told a *Los Angeles Times* reporter: "I knew The Eagles were over half way through 'The Long Run'.

I could give you 30 reasons why but let me be concise about it. I started the band, I got tired of it and I quit."

Henley, in 1989, was candid about at least one of Frey's 30 reasons for the band's demise. "Walsh was an insidious troublemaker. He was one of the reasons why the band broke up. He was always splitting the band into factions."

Frey, in a subsequent interview, seemed more angry than saddened by the break-up. "I will never have the patience to deal with all those kinds of personalities again. But at the time it was necessary to get to where we had to go, even though we didn't always get along."

On the eve of The Eagles reunion tour, however, he appeared to have put the past far enough behind him to deal with the subject even more candidly. "We always had to worry about doing this or living up to that. So much time has passed now that I'm not really mad at the guys I was really mad at. The Eagles just became like an ongoing nightmare towards the end.

"I hesitate to blame it all on drugs because that's such an easy excuse," he continued. "But it is fair to say that cocaine may have brought out the worst in some of us. But what really got to us was that the band just got bigger and bigger and it just became totally unmanageable. There was the burden to follow things up and I think we just ran out of gas.

"We had done a lot within the confines of a five piece band but musically it was probably time for us to work with other people. In a twisted sort of way, having the bird's nest full of hand grenades on the live album was probably our way of telling ourselves that."

Felder cut even deeper to the heart of the band's problems when he said: "Everybody wanted two songs on each album but sometimes it just turned out to be better to have six Don Henley songs on an album. And that didn't make a lot of people happy."

Henley never seemed too far away from the heart of the problem, the creative struggles within the band. "Everybody in The Eagles has a particular gift and everybody in The Eagles is good at something. But what everybody did not realise is that you can't do everything.

That's when the egos started getting in the way and that's when we started having trouble." But ultimately he claimed that, creatively, the band was the better for all the fussing and fighting. "We still managed to get through eight years of thrashing and disagreeing and we still managed to create a lot out of that. That was the important thing."

Meanwhile, the individual 'Eagles' continued their habit of appearing on records by others, Henley, Schmit and Walsh on Karla Bonoff's 'Wild Heart Of The Young', and Schmit, not surprisingly, on 'Toto IV'.

It wasn't until May of 1982 that manager Irving Azoff finally made things official, announcing in a short press release that The Eagles had officially disbanded. In later years he would look back on the break-up as a good thing. "By then they were in their early thirties. They had built houses, made tons of money, but they had never really had the time off to enjoy it. So there were lots of reasons to back off from the pressure. One day they just kind of drifted into divorce. But I still think that some day they will collaborate again."

Henley, looking back on those times in a 1990 interview, was not so sure. "As far as I was concerned the well was dry. It was simply dry."

Chapter X

Nobody Just Retires

"We always knew that he (Bernie) wouldn't just retire completely," said Henley in 1977. "He just wanted to do things at his own pace." Don Henley was talking specifically about Bernie Leadon, but he could just as easily have been summing up all of the former Eagles and the paths they took following the band's official demise.

Leadon turned out to be the first of them to put forth a solo effort when, in the summer of 1977, he teamed with Michael Georgiades to release the album 'Natural Progressions' which ended up barely cracking the Top 100 at No. 91. Prior to this less than glorious début, Leadon had wasted little time getting into session work by appearing on Chris Hillman's 'Slippin' Away' which was released in February 1976.

Walsh, ever prolific, had released his first solo LP as an Eagle with the live 'You Can't Argue With A Sick Mind' which topped out at No. 20. In May 1978, he unleashed the solo 'But Seriously Folks' which went platinum *en route* to a No. 8 chart listing and produced the amusingly autobiographical 'Life's Been Good' which reached No. 12.

That same month the soundtrack for the movie *FM* hit stores, went to No. 5 and went platinum, and, with the song 'Bad Man', announced the beginning of Randy Meisner's solo career which continued in June with the release of his first full length solo album 'Randy Meisner'.

"When I left The Eagles, I decided to do an album right away," remembers Meisner. "I didn't have any songs written and so I just put a bunch of things together just to be able to do an album."

Meisner, still managed by Irving Azoff, watched sadly as his solo début failed to find any foothold on the charts. Musically, Meisner seemed to know the reason why when looking back in 1981. "The album had too many ballads," he lamented. "They were too long and too repetitive."

Meisner was not thrilled. He was even less thrilled when, after a tour financed largely out of his own pocket failed to ignite sales, he dropped by Azoff's office to get some questions answered. "I was wondering why we weren't getting any airplay and I was getting a little frustrated so I went to see Irving. He went crazy and started shouting at me all the way down the stairs. He said 'Get the hell out of here! You're done!'

Later I found out that Don and Glenn had called Irving and said that if he was going to manage me, they were going to find other management."

Meisner's woes continued. Elektra dropped him from the label around the same time that Azoff showed him the door. "Irving was too busy for me and Elektra didn't have any faith in me. That really hurt. When that first album didn't work out I was shattered. I went back to Nebraska. I was all set to retire."

Back home, Meisner drank a lot, rode his motorcycle around the flat countryside and sat around doing nothing at all, and nothing musical in particular. Even at his lowest point, he was not immune to the boredom that was setting in. "I could just ride around on a motorcycle and drink beer for so long," he says.

Meanwhile Leadon, always more comfortable in group situations than on his own, became, in 1978, part of the team that produced an ambitious concept LP called 'White Mansions: A Tale Of The American Civil War 1861-1865'. The album, produced by former Eagles' producer Glyn Johns, featured Leadon on a number of stringed instruments, but it never charted and quickly disappeared. But Leadon continued to stay active and, in 1980, had the last laugh on his former band when his instrumental piece 'Journey Of The Sorcerer', the instrumental track championed by producer Szymczyk on 'One Of These Nights', was picked up in the United Kingdom as the theme music for the television series *The Hitchhiker's Guide To The Galaxy*.

In the meantime, Meisner slowly but surely regained his interest in music. He returned to Los Angeles in 1980 in an attempt to interest another label but discovered that nobody was interested in a former Eagle who was 0 for 1 on his own. "There were so many disappointments, I almost gave up again and went back to Nebraska."

Eventually, though, he secured new management and was offered a contract by Epic Records. He returned to the studio in a more relaxed frame of mind and, in October 1980, released a second solo LP entitled 'One More Song'. The album only reached No. 50 on the charts but enjoyed a longer than expected shelf life thanks to three chart singles:

'Deep Inside My Heart' which hit No. 22, 'Hearts On Fire' which cracked the Top 20 and 'Gotta Get Away' at No. 83. By this time Meisner had buried the hatchet with Frey and Henley and they sang background vocals on the last song.

Shortly after the release of 'One More Song', Meisner told the *Los Angeles Times* that, despite all the years in all the bands, he was still learning the ropes. "I'm still learning. Occasionally I'll forget lyrics and I guess I'm not always the most exciting live act. But remember, I was always in the background. Coming out of the background isn't easy. It's certainly harder than I thought it would be."

Meisner toured with the album and, with his divorce recently final, found himself going through some unpleasant changes. "I was drinking a lot of booze, a lot of hard liquor and that would get me into a lot of trouble. I was getting drunk and tipping as big as I could. I was being foolish and I was going through a lot of money."

'The Long Run' followed Meisner's record out in 1980 and, looking in on The Eagles from the outside for the first time, he did not think much of it. "'The Long Run' was nothing to brag about as far as I was concerned. It was a little too straight and sterile sounding as far as I was concerned. But then I didn't give a shit at that point and they probably didn't either."

May 15, 1981 saw the release of yet another Walsh solo LP, 'There Goes The Neighborhood', which went to No. 20 on the album charts and produced the No. 4 chart single 'A Life Of Illusion'. Don Felder joined the solo parade in July with two songs on the soundtrack for the movie *Heavy Metal*. Felder's song 'All Of You' was a standout album track while his 'Heavy Metal (Takin' A Ride)' hit No. 43 on the singles charts.

Felder was humble in response to this modest success in a 1981 *LA Times* interview. "I'm not a solo artist *per se*," he commented. "There's no master plan to go out on my own. What happened with those songs was totally unexpected. It just slipped up on me. Everybody in The Eagles has kept a low profile so that we could remain a band instead of waving our own flags. This is the first exposure I've really had."

He was quick to point out that a chart single did not necessarily mean Felder as a solo artist would soon be out there. "It's comfortable being in The Eagles because it's a team of players and you can hide in there. But I'm real happy and excited that the single is doing well. It makes me want to make more."

But these contributions were essentially the opening act for what Eagles' fans felt would be the main event, the first solo releases by Henley and Frey. They did not have to wait long – a mere three weeks after the official announcement of The Eagles disbanding, on May 28, 1982, Glenn Frey's first solo effort, 'No Fun Allowed', was released. It was an album more concerned with pop sensibilities and a party atmosphere than with Eagles' style harmonies and political and social concerns. Much of the change can be attributed to the fact that Frey shares songwriting on six of the ten tracks with occasional Eagles contributor Jack Tempchin, a solid tunesmith not known for his political and social lyrics.

Frey explained in a post-'No Fun Allowed' interview that the songwriting and recording process for that album was, by comparison to past Eagles' efforts, leisurely. "I had no intention of killing myself on this album. I was spending about eight hours in the studio and then basically calling it quits for the day. I discovered over the years that, after about eight hours, you start not getting returns and so you're better off stopping at a point where you're doing well so you always want to go back to work the next day. And when I was in the studio, I was doing what felt good to me.

"This was a busting loose album for me," he continued. "I cut a couple of oldies; it was all pretty light-hearted."

According to Frey, the light-hearted nature of 'No Fun Allowed' was a vinyl response to the stress he had suffered towards the end of The Eagles' run. "The Eagles were thought of as serious and rightfully so. Things got real serious after 'Hotel California' and I didn't want things that way on this album."

For his part, Henley was not surprised that his former partner was taking it easy. "I think Glenn just got tired of how serious and worrisome it all was and he wanted to have a good time. I really think he'd had a belly full of it by the time The Eagles were over and just wanted to relax and enjoy it. And if that's his way of enjoying it, fine."

'No Fun Allowed' was not the immediate hit one might have expected from its predominant voice. In fact, the album took seven months to inch up to gold status and only went as high as No. 32 on the album list. The first single off the album, 'I Found Somebody', made it to No. 31, followed by 'The One You Love' which reached No. 15 and 'All Those Lies' which bogged down at No. 41.

August, 1982, saw the release of Randy Meisner's third LP. The album, his second to be entitled 'Randy Meisner', featured the Elton John song 'Strangers' sung as a duet by Meisner and Heart's Ann Wilson, but it failed to duplicate the success of its predecessor; reaching No. 94 on the charts and producing the single 'Never Been In Love' which went to No. 28. "We had a lot of good songs and good players on that album but I think we went in the wrong direction by trying to be a little bit heavier," said Meisner later.

Henley, Schmit, Felder and Walsh all managed to get songs on the 1982 movie soundtrack for *Fast Times At Ridgemont High* which rose to No. 54 on the charts. Schmit's cover of The Tymes' hit 'So Much In Love' was the closest thing to an ex-Eagles' hit, going to No. 59 on the singles list.

Meanwhile, lurking in the background, Don Henley was putting the finishing touches to his début solo album, 'I Can't Stand Still', and taking his first tentative steps into an uncluttered spotlight. Following The Eagles' break-up he'd spent his time drinking, doing cocaine, playing the recluse and dealing with a drug related arrest. The sudden and total lack of communication between Frey and himself was also difficult to deal with after so long.

"I knew what it meant," Henley reflected in 1991. "I was going to have to do the same thing. Some of the other guys wanted to go on as The

Eagles without Glenn which was really ridiculous. I was scared a little bit... no I was scared a lot.

"But finally I picked myself up off the floor and said 'Okay damn it! I'm going to do this and nobody and nothing is going to stop me'."

Feeling unable to do it alone, he hooked up with guitarist-songwriter Danny Kortchmar, the LA session veteran who would be more than able to deal with Henley's meticulous studio manner. Over the years Kortchmar had worked his magic for Jackson Browne, Carole King and James Taylor, and Henley's offer was particularly enticing. "I was getting the chance to produce," he said. "We were trying to create a sound from scratch. What instruments will work and what won't? What would the background vocals be like? Don was offering me the kind of freedom I'd never had with any artist."

Kortchmar ended up with a writing credit on eight of the 11 songs on an album that also included musical and vocal support from Schmit, Walsh and the sixth Eagle J.D. Souther.

But Henley's plans were marred by personal tragedy when his long-time girlfriend, actress Maren Jensen, came down with what was then considered the mysterious malady Epstein-Barr Syndrome. Jensen, who stayed with Henley until February 1986, related, in *GQ,* that those were trying times for both of them. "It was a really tough period in my life as well as his. I was so young and to have so many things bombarding me all at once... it was overwhelming. But we hung in there. We had a lot of love for each other."

Henley agreed with Jensen. "I stood by her and she stood by me." But he was candid about the pressures and uncertainties of launching his solo career and caring for Jensen.

"I was freaked out," he said. "I was attentive and supportive but I didn't exactly come home when I was supposed to because I was traumatised. Kootch and I would record until three in the morning and then come back to my house and guzzle Scotch and Vodka and tell each other how great we were."

'I Can't Stand Still' was released on August 13, 1982, and became an immediate critics' favourite due, in large amount, to such politically and socially responsible songs as 'Johnny Can't Read' and 'Dirty Laundry'. The album went to No. 24 on the charts and was ultimately certified gold. The first single, 'Johnny Can't Read' only made it to No. 42 but, the follow up 'Dirty Laundry' climbed all the way to No. 3 and, likewise, went gold. A third single, the more playful 'I Can't Stand Still', stalled at No. 48.

Always the deepest thinker in The Eagles and certainly the most socially aware, Henley took pains to emphasise the importance of songs like 'Dirty Laundry', which takes shots at the crass nature of the tabloid media. "I'm a citizen and a tax payer just like everybody else and I feel I'm entitled to some privacy and some dignity. I figure I owe my fans the best songs I can write, the best records I can make and the best performances I can give. Other than that I feel like my life should be my own."

Timothy Schmit was particularly active on the session front during the summer of 1982, contributing vocals to the Eye To Eye album of the same name, the Crosby, Stills And Nash album 'Daylight Again', and America's 'View From The Ground'. Henley, during his busy solo season, managed to squeeze in singing duties on Warren Zevon's 'The Envoy'.

Over at Asylum Records the men that balance the accounts were far from satisfied with the money – or lack of it – now being generated by former Eagles. It therefore came as little surprise when they unveiled plans for an end of the year release of 'Eagles Greatest Hits Vol. 2'.

Easily the most exploitative scar on The Eagles' discography, 'Greatest Hits Volume 2' repackages elements of 'Hotel California' and 'The Long Run' into a truncated collection that has no rhyme or reason other than to squeeze a little more money out of The Eagles' legacy. The band was upset by it, and so was every self-respecting fan.

Henley, looking back on that LP in 1989, was not amused. "That album only had two albums of songs to draw on so it wasn't much of a greatest hits album. It was a big rip-off as far as I'm concerned."

A big rip off that, nonetheless, went gold not too long after its December 1982 release while reaching a relatively disappointing No. 52 on the charts. The year ended with Felder and Frey tuning up their guitars on Bob Seger's album 'The Distance'.

The following year was slow on Eagles related activities. Early in the Spring Henley sang on the Christopher Cross LP 'Another Page'. Walsh was in the review columns again in June with another solo outing, 'You Bought It... You Name It' which climbed to No. 48 and let loose the single 'Space Age Whiz Kids' which scaled the charts to No. 52. Eagles music was also proving attractive to other artists and in September the Willie Nelson-Waylon Jennings duet on 'Take It To The Limit' crossed over to a No. 8 birth on the country charts. November saw Don Felder entering the solo follies with the album 'Airborne' which bombed out at No. 178 on the charts. This was his first and last solo effort to date.

Meanwhile Frey, whose relationship with the Asylum label had deteriorated since chief executive Joe Smith had left the company, was meeting with his new bosses and finding that the situation was deteriorating still further. "The people who took over Asylum made it known in their first interviews that they weren't particularly interested in having the company become a country rock graveyard. They had no sense of history and didn't care for the fact that The Eagles, Linda Ronstadt, Jackson Browne and Joni Mitchell had basically built that company."

Matters came to a head when Frey, who concedes that he should have known better, delivered the tapes of his second solo album 'The Allnighter'. "They passed on it," recalled an astonished Frey in a *Billboard* interview. "They said it wasn't contemporary enough. I was angry but I went back and cut three more songs because I felt it was time to write a couple of hits."

But rather than rush the additional songs back to Asylum, Frey took a long hard look at his future with the label. "I don't think they ever had any serious thought about keeping me. I think they would have found any number of ways to make it uncomfortable for me, to make me want to leave. Rather than have Asylum take my record and not do anything with it, I wanted to have somebody who thought it was good and wanted to work it. That's why I felt it was time to move on."

Frey moved on to MCA Records where Irving Azoff was now Company President. When his second solo LP, 'The Allnighter', was released in June 1984, it bettered 'No Fun Allowed' by staying on the charts 65 weeks and topping out at No. 22. The first single off the album, 'Sexy Girl' crashed the Top 20 but the follow up, 'The Allnighter', struggled to No. 54.

Frey was nevertheless very happy with the album. "I put a lot more thought into the new album," he said. "The themes of the songs are a little more provocative and involved. The songs on this album, and on all my albums for that matter, tend to grow on people. Like warts."

Shortly after the release of 'The Allnighter' he conceded to a *Musician* interviewer that he was beginning to find his chops as a lead guitarist and explained why the transformation to budding guitar hero had to wait this long. "Not taking lead real often with The Eagles was pretty much my own choosing. After Bernie left, my role as a singer became much more important and so I had to concentrate on being in tune all the time. Besides, I felt it was more important for The Eagles that we get a couple of blistering guitarists in there. I was the one who drafted Walsh and Felder.

"But then I figured at that time what better way is there to learn how to play guitar than to play with people who are better than you are," he continued. "It didn't do me too bad to be playing with the Joe Walsh's, the Don Felders and the Bernie Leadons of the world. In fact I'd call that pretty smart."

Critically the consensus was that Frey, two albums on, was having a hard time getting serious which resulted in music that, while infectious, was basically lightweight fare. Frey was mum on the subject but Henley leaped to his former partner's defence. "He wanted to do something he enjoyed and he wanted to play the kind of music he enjoyed, which is rhythm and blues, soul and Memphis music. This is the stuff he loves so I don't know what the problem is."

Frey maintained that although his solo material met with little commercial success, especially compared to The Eagles, he was happy to be in a situation... "where I'm not always being asked when I'm going to get The Eagles back together again and I'm dealing with people who are actually interested in my solo career. I want to give my solo career a good shot; a fair and decent chance. I don't think you just throw up your arms in panic when the first album doesn't go platinum."

And the one thing Frey, at this point, had no intention of entertaining, was going back to the safety net of The Eagles. "I think when you're in your twenties, it's good to be in a band. You like to band together with other people until you can get on your feet. But I'm in my thirties now. I want to step out and be my own person. I don't expect to do as well as The Eagles did in terms of sales. That's not my goal. My goal is to develop as an artist and a writer."

Henley also swapped labels in 1984, moving from Asylum to Geffen. Like Frey, his reasoning was his never ending battle of art *vs* commerce. "When David (Geffen) left it (Asylum) became this huge, gaping thing with lots of artists," he lamented. "They were using the money that The Eagles and Jackson Browne and Linda Ronstadt made to sign up all these shit artists. And then they started to say 'You guys have got to give us more albums. Hurry up! You're fucking things up! Our quarterly report is not going to look so good'."

In November Henley released his second album 'Building The Perfect Beast', a record that painted some real life pictures but, unlike its predecessor, was not drawn as much from Henley's own life. "I'm sort of learning how to make things up," he said shortly after the release of the record. "I'm writing about things as I see them but it's not necessarily something that happened to me. I'm thankful that it all doesn't have to be personal experience any more. It was getting a little rough."

'Building The Perfect Beast' catapulted to No. 13 and quickly went platinum. The first single, 'The Boys Of Summer' went to No. 5. The follow up song 'All She Wants To Do Is Dance' hit No. 9, while the third single 'Not Enough Love In The World' got to No. 34. A fourth single, 'Sunset Grill' rose to No. 22.

Henley's popularity stretched overseas and he travelled to England in 1985 for a round of press for 'Beast'. Although he was making great strides in leaving his sour puss image behind, the tone of the questions facing him that year were often serious in content, requiring like responses. "'Building The Perfect Beast' is more than a title for an album," he acknowledged to one interviewer. "It's the overriding theme of these songs. It's the way I see us going. We've got a Star Wars technology and we can genetically engineer what our kids are going to look like. But we still don't treat each other any better than we did several centuries ago. We haven't advanced in that direction at all, as individuals or as nations."

Though he was keen to distance himself from The Eagles and concentrate on promoting his own work, the inevitable Eagles questions cropped up during his overseas jaunt. Journalists were anxious to find out what broke the band up, and Henley was candid in his replies. "The group was breaking up from the day it got together," he told a *Melody Maker* reporter. "There were always conflicts there as there are in any group. The Eagles died of natural causes for exactly the same reasons as any group splits.

"I want to sing more songs. You sing more than me. You write more than me. You know, that kind of thing. Some of us wanted to do benefits for certain charities and others didn't. Some of us wanted to tour longer than others. It was the usual things that broke us up; jealousy, envy and greed."

It was also during his England jaunt that Henley addressed the issue of survival, not so much the survival of being in a supergroup like The Eagles but of the survival of the spirit and the flesh. "I made it through the Seventies alive and with my brain reasonably intact," he chuckled, "and I know that surprises a lot of people. From the rumours that have gone around, I think most people expect us all to be a bunch of complete derelicts. And make no mistake, we had our moments. We had our benders and our binges. We did our share of every substance known to man. But we all came through it in reasonably good shape and I see no reason for us to stop as long as our music remains viable and valid."

In the race for ex-Eagles commercial viability, Henley was closing out 1984 a full lap up on Frey. But Frey managed a comeback of major proportions in December when his song 'The Heat Is On' jumped off the *Beverly Hills Cop* movie soundtrack and clawed its way to No. 2 on the singles charts by March 16, 1985, making 'Heat' the highest ranking single by an ex-Eagle. Schmit entered the solo fray in October with the album 'Playin' It Cool', a commercial washout which went no higher than No. 160 on the charts, and he rounded out 1984 with a guest appearance on Dan Fogelberg's LP 'Windows And Walls'. Schmit and Henley appeared on J.D. Souther's 'Home By Dawn' and Leadon on Chris Hillman's 'Desert Rose' album.

Although the competition between Frey and Henley was largely unspoken, the pair seemed to have a knack for not letting each other pull too far out in front. The success had hardly dried on Frey's *Beverly Hills Cop* when Henley, early in 1985, emerged with the song 'She's On The Zoom' on the soundtrack for the movie *Vision Quest* which made it to platinum status, as did 'Cop', and a No. 11 album position.

1985 was also the year that Frey guested in an episode of the television series *Miami Vice* which was based on the story of intrigue told in Frey's song 'Smuggler's Blues'. Capitalising on his acting début, Frey's record company released 'Smuggler's Blues' as a single and watched quite happily as it not only soared to No. 12 but also revived interest in the slowly sinking 'The Allnighter' album. This second chance resulted in increased sales and a gold record by August of the same year.

Joe Walsh recorded albums to a production line schedule and in the spring of 1985 there emerged yet another new LP entitled 'The Confessor'. But not even a tour opening for Tina Turner could prevent this from being one of Walsh's least successful, rising only to No. 65.

Walsh's other contribution to the music world in 1985 was playing guitar on Michael McDonald's 'No Lookin' Back' album.

The remainder of the year was rounded out by still more soundtrack contributions. Felder and Schmit contributed songs to the *Secret Admirer* soundtrack which did only moderate business. Frey's contribution to the *Miami Vice* television soundtrack, 'You Belong To The City', went to No. 2 on the singles list.

1986 was easily the most barren year for ex-Eagles projects. Songwriting, the occasional tour and more of that hard-to-get-used-to leisure time kept most of the group members out of the limelight. In fact, the only noise during the year was made by Henley who, in February, won a Grammy for Best Rock Performance Male for his song 'The Boys Of Summer'. Later in the year he contributed the song 'Who Owns This Place' to the soundtrack for *The Color Of Money*.

Frey flexed his acting muscles again in 1987 with a supporting role in the mercenaries *versus* drug cartel action film *Let's Get Harry* (aka *The Rescue*) opposite Robert Duvall and Gary Busey. How good Frey actually was in the film is a bit of a mystery as the film was never released in theatres and is reportedly hard to find on video shelves. But the experience inspired Frey to temporarily step away from the music and attempt to play the acting game. "I went out for interviews for other feature films," he said in 1993, wincing at the memory, "but found the whole cattle call process too demeaning."

Early in the year Bernie Leadon joined The Nitty Gritty Dirt Band, replacing group leader John McEuen as a touring and recording member. Walsh trotted out yet another album during the summer, 'Got Any Gum?' which settled in at No. 113. Schmit, months later, released his second solo LP 'Timothy B.' which went to No. 106 on the album charts and produced two chart singles; 'Boys' Night Out' at No. 25 and 'Don't Give Up' which reached No. 30.

Four years after his last album, Glenn Frey released his third album 'Soul Searchin'' in the summer of 1988. Frey continued to struggle as a solo artist; his album was only moderately successful at No. 36. The first single off the album, 'True Love', reached No. 13. A second single 'Soul Searchin'' was a pop chart miss but crawled up the Adult Contemporary charts to No. 5. The third single off the album, 'Livin' Right' went nowhere at No. 90. Frey salved his disappointment by turning to acting again and received high marks for his role as a burned out record company executive on the television series *Wiseguy*.

Walsh returned to the soundtrack wars with a song on 'The Great Outdoors' album while Leadon, as a member of The Nitty Gritty Dirt Band, had a No. 33 berth on the country charts with the album 'Workin' Band'. Leadon also ushered in Spring 1989 as a part of the Dirt Band's 'Will The Circle Be Unbroken, Vol. 2'.

Throughout the decade the subject of an Eagles' reunion was a constant question on any solo promotional junket. Frey and Henley usually dismissed the question out of hand. But occasionally other members of the band would express a desire for a reunion or a sadness that the band split apart in the first place.

Felder, in an interview during the Eighties, said "I would have preferred to have stayed with The Eagles."

Schmit took it a little more personally. "I went around for a long time after the break-up, changing the radio station when Eagles' songs came on because it was sad to think what had happened."

Henley, five years after 'Building The Perfect Beast', released his third solo album, 'The End Of The Innocence'. This was a breakthrough album in the sense that Henley, long an apparent slave to the limits of a pop audience, pushed the demographics as many of the songs from the album crossed over to adult radio playlists. The first single out of the box, 'The End Of The Innocence', went to No. 8 on the pop charts but leapt to No. 2 on the adult contemporary listings. 'The Last Worthless Evening' was second out of the box and was, likewise, a two pronged winner with placement on both the pop (No. 21) and adult (No. 2) charts. A third single, 'The Heart Of The Matter', also did the two bagger with a No. 21 pop finish and a No. 3 adult bulleting. Henley suffered a temporary blip when a fourth single, 'How Bad Do You Want It?' only reached No. 48 pop with no crossover action but a fifth single, 'New York Minute' recaptured the magic with a No. 48 pop and No. 5 adult finish.

'The End Of The Innocence' ultimately topped out at No. 8 on the LP charts but managed to hang around an almost unprecedented 148 weeks and, on that initial sales burst, went triple platinum. Henley, obviously in a good space, used the occasion to comment on the fact that, to this day, he still gets mistaken for Glenn Frey. "People have short attention spans and memories," he noted in *Time*. "They forget me as soon as I'm off MTV. I'm glad."

Henley also speculated on how The Eagles' music would stand the test of time. "The Eagles were another link in the chain, a logical extension of what came before. But I don't think the Seventies will ever be as important in the history of rock as the Sixties because you don't have the cultural and sociological upheaval combined with the music."

While Henley was in outer space, Walsh was having fun in the summer of 1989 as part of Ringo Starr's touring All Star Band. For the record, Walsh sang 'Life In The Fast Lane' during the tour on a regular basis and was enshrined on a live LP of the show that came out in 1990. In August 1989 Randy Meisner, who had been out of the recording-touring loop since 1982, mended fences with the original line-up of Poco and rejoined the band for a new LP 'Legacy' which, ironically, became the band's first album to go gold (No. 40 on the charts) and a series of tours that lasted through summer 1990. Meisner left Poco at that point and, in the fall of 1990, hooked up with a country band called Black Tie whose cover of the Buddy Holly song called 'Learning The Game' made No. 59 in the country charts.

Henley captured a second Grammy for Best Rock Vocal Performance for 'The End Of The Innocence' in 1990, but things were not going nearly so well for the luckless Schmit. In July 1990, his third solo album 'Tell Me The Truth' failed to chart at all and Schmit subsequently retreated into session and touring work ,with his most notable appearance of 1990 being as part of Jimmy Buffett's backup band.

Frey continued his romance with the soundtrack in the Spring of 1991 as the song 'Part Of Me, Part Of You' made its way into *Thelma And Louise*. Very much in the mould of The Eagles, it went Top 10 on the rock and adult charts but tumbled to No. 55 on the pop line. Also available in spring of 1991 was yet another album by the prolific Walsh, 'Ordinary Average Guy' which ended up lodged in the depths at No. 112. The title track proved more potent, cracking the Top 10.

Former Eagles continued to pick up the pace in 1992. A trio called The Remingtons, featuring Bernie Leadon, released the album 'Blue Frontier' in January and struggled to No. 55 on the country charts. Walsh and Schmit teamed up with Ringo in June for another round of tours with his All Starr Band that lasted until August. Henley, whose social commitment had turned in the direction of preserving the woods around Walden Pond in Massachusetts, headlined two benefit concerts in March and April that saw him performing with Clint Black, Neil Young, John Fogerty and Roger Waters. A highlight of those shows was Black and Henley singing Eagles' songs together. The intrigue further thickened when Black announced that Henley and he would be writing songs together for his next album. But when the Black album 'The Hard Way' was released on July 14, it contained no songs credited to Henley.

Randy Meisner and his band Black Tie gave it one more shot in May with a cover of country star Nanci Griffith's 'Listen To The Radio' that did not chart. The band hit rock bottom. But, happily, Meisner was on the way back. "I had been real foolish with the money and the booze and finally, some years back, it was like Kaboom!," he reflected. "I didn't have any more money. So I decided I've got to get a hold of this or I'm going all the way down. So I cleaned up my personal habits, got a hold of a good accountant and basically caught myself in time. Today I'm sitting pretty good."

Frey thought he was sitting pretty good when his fourth solo outing, 'Strange Weather' was released on June 23. But the album proved to be one of the major disappointments in Frey's life when it failed to find the charts. Salvaging some semblance of pride were the singles 'I've Got

Mine' (which peaked at No. 12 on the adult charts and died at No. 91 on the pop charts) and 'River Of Dreams' which stalled at No. 27 on the adult charts.

That same month Henley added his distinctive vocal shadings to the single 'Sometimes Love Just Ain't Enough' on the self titled album by Patty Smyth. In August of that year, Joe Walsh trotted out yet another platter, 'Songs For A Dying Planet'. The first single off the album, 'Vote For Me', went to No. 10 on the album rock tracks list. A second song off the album, 'Shut Up', is notable for mentioning Frey and Henley by name and borrowing a guitar lick from 'Life In The Fast Lane'.

The September release of 'Amused To Death', a solo LP by former Pink Floyd linchpin Roger Waters, was conspicuous by a duet between Waters and Henley on the track 'Watching TV'. October saw the release of 'Big Iron Horses' by Bernie Leadon's band Restless Heart which went to No. 26 on the country charts and No. 116 on the pop list.

Early in 1993, with his solo career sluggish at best, Frey was preparing a musical change of pace. Spurred on by the apparent success of the 'Common Ground' album, Frey had his heart set on a musical trip to Nashville. "It would have been real safe for me to go to Nashville and make a country rock record, which is what I was going to do," he said.

But fate once again stepped in with an acting offer to play a hip private eye in a weekly television series called *South Of Sunset*. "We had been looking and looking for four months for a lead before the idea of calling Frey was hit upon," reported series co-producer Stan Rogow. "With Glenn there's frankly stuff that actors couldn't pull off – which is his *persona*. If an actor tries to act cool it just seems silly. Glenn is cool. What he brings to the party is something that would almost not be obtainable."

Rogow and his partner John Byrum subsequently met with Frey to sound him out on taking the role. "When we sat down to talk with Glenn about it, he had already read the script and he said 'So I get it. The show is about the tarnished elegance of Los Angeles.' And I said 'Well yeah.' We could see immediately that it would be a perfect match."

Frey immediately jumped at the opportunity to tackle something a bit more risky than a country music album. "This is a real whoa!" he said just after filming began on the series. "I'm dumb enough to just wade right in there, just dive right in and say 'Okay. I'll try!' Where's the cliff again? How far do I jump?"

Frey jumped right in but, as he continued to crank out the episodes in advance of the October 27 début, he began to have doubts. Finally, just prior to the airing of the pilot, Frey faxed off an angry message to a number of television and studio executives saying, in the calm before the storm, that the pilot episode was weak and that the first episode after the pilot was a more appropriate introduction to the series. Already aware that the network was intent on airing the pilot, he concluded his message with... "This is the most gutless, tasteless, chickenshit movie I've ever seen."

The tirade, according to one person close to the *South Of Sunset* problems, was "Because he is not a seasoned TV actor, Glenn isn't aware of what it takes to get a show on the air and keep it there."

Frey got hot and bothered once again, firing off more nasty missives when the promo spots for the show began airing as the début episode neared its broadcast date. "They weren't right for the show," he said. "So I had to tell some people and they listened. Because I'm the star, it's very important that I look good and come off the way we want me to come off which is genuine, not a yuckster. To look at the promos you'd think it was a comedy show and I'm not doing *The Keystone Kops*."

Eight episodes of the series had been filmed, but when the pilot episode was savagely attacked by critics and largely ignored by viewers, the network stepped in and cancelled the show on the spot. Co-producer Rogow, however, insisted during a post- mortem captured by *Entertainment Weekly* that Frey's fax tantrum had nothing to do with the cancellation. "We were opposite *Home Improvement* and *Melrose Place*," he sighed. "We could have aired *Gone With The Wind* and no one would have watched."

Frey finally mellowed on the subject to pick up the tab for the wrap party for *South Of Sunset* at which he and Joe Walsh performed. The theme of the party was 'You can't cancel rock and roll.'

But you could most certainly die of non-support as Frey also discovered in 1993 when his live LP 'Glenn Frey Live' went out with even less record company support than 'Strange Weather' and sank like the proverbial stone.

Walsh, with something to prove after his last two Pyramid albums failed to pack a Top 40 punch, was continuing to be active on the soundtrack front even as The Eagles were making their first tentative steps toward re-forming. In 1994 he teamed with progressive country star Steven Earle on the song 'Honey Don't' on *The Beverly Hillbillies* soundtrack. And, early in 95, alongside Lita Ford, Frankie Miller and Nicky Hopkins, he was featured on the *Robocop* TV series soundtrack, entitled 'Robocop: A Future...' with the songs 'A Future To This Life', 'Guilty Of A Crime' and 'Fire and Brimstone'.

Frey's disastrous relationship with MCA continued when he issued a greatest hits package from his solo catalogue entitled 'Solo Collection' which, like its predecessors, was attracting no interest from record buyers early in 1995. Given Frey's continual failure as a solo artist and the lacklustre solo careers of most of the other members, it's not surprising that Frey and Henley were continually having to deal with questions about an Eagles' reunion. And, recalled Frey in looking back on those often less than spectacular solo years, the push wasn't always from the fans.

"Every couple of years I would run into Irving Azoff and he'd go 'You know, there is a bushel basket of $100 bills waiting for you if you guys could just get together and do an album or a tour.' But I'd go 'Yes but I have a nice life now. It's not that important to me'."

Azoff continued to believe that an Eagles' reunion would happen some day, though he understood that money wouldn't be a motive. "I still believe that some day they'll collaborate again," he said. "Many other bands have come back for reunion shot after reunion shot. They take the money and run. Glenn and Don won't do that which should tell you something about their integrity."

Henley, recounting that period in 1994, claimed he was ambivalent about the questions and the offers. "I went in cycles about the whole thing," he insisted. "There were times when I thought 'Never! Not even if they begged me! ' And then there were times where I would think 'Well maybe it wouldn't be so bad'."

Chapter XI

Time Passes, Things Change

Late in 1984 Don Henley was sitting up one night in front of the television set, unwinding after a long day of writing and promoting for 'Building The Perfect Beast'. *Late Night With David Letterman* flickered across the screen. The announcer came on with the night's guest line-up. "And Glenn Frey!"

Henley perked up. He watched Frey perform and make inane small talk with Letterman. Long after the show ended Henley remained deep in thought, deep in memories.

The next day Henley rang Frey up just to say hi. They began to talk and, as they talked they began to put a lot of the bitterness behind them. Finally on New Year's Day 1985, the pair got together in Aspen, Colorado for a face-to-face meeting. They talked for hours amid the snowy, quiet confines of their retreat and came to a bit of an understanding. And a very cautious commitment to maybe try and write together again sometime.

In a post-Aspen interview in *Rolling Stone*, Henley indicated, "It's a possibility that Glenn and I will work together again. But there is a certain amount of worry that any music we might make together would be scrutinised unbearably hard."

Frey, for his part, indicated that the reason for Don and he not communicating in the previous years was more professional than personal. "The reason Don and I don't talk so much is because The Eagles were our common interest and not because of any real falling out between us."

But Henley also admitted that those early telephone conversations and get togethers did do a lot to clear the air. "In some ways I think a lot of the conflict was imaginary. We were apart and the rumours would get back to us about something the other guy might have said and it might set us off. But every time we were actually in each other's presence everything was fine. Every time we would run into each other, there was no bitterness or animosity."

While peace between Frey and Henley appeared to have been made by the mid-Eighties, the idea of working together and possibly working together as The Eagles still seemed remote. Since the break-up Frey had been offered big money on two occasions to do an Eagles reunion at US Festivals but turned them down. As far as new Eagles' product was concerned, Frey once told *Billboard* magazine, "If The Eagles were to fart in a bag, the label would have tried to get a stereo mix and ask me what I wanted on the B- side."

Once Frey's dry humour left him, he was usually left explaining how it could happen and why it most likely would not. "If The Eagles were to get back together, it would have to be for the right reasons," he told *Musician* in the mid Eighties. "I think it would look awful if we just did it for the money. The US Festival twice offered us a lot of money but money's not an issue. But I think it's an issue for the people who want to put The Eagles back together. I know money is not an issue for Don."

Henley, as the years passed, began to take the possibility of an Eagles' reunion or, at the very least, another writing project with Frey, more seriously. "The thoughts of possibly doing it again kept going around for years. I don't think I ever totally discounted the possibility of it. As our friend J.D. Souther always used to say, 'Time passes, things change'."

The first real hint of an Eagles' reunion came about early in 1990 when Frey and Henley agreed to get together and write a few original songs as an added bonus for a projected Eagles Greatest Hits package. *Rolling Stone* caught up with the pair in Los Angeles that same year and posed the question on everybody's mind. What does it feel like to be working together again?

"Well, we're going to see what happens," said Frey. "It will be interesting. There's certainly a lot to write about."

Henley added: "I think we've matured a great deal. We have a better perspective on the world and our place in it."

And the pair appeared more comfortable than ever before with the idea of an Eagles' reunion. "I just decided to be open to the possibilities," said Frey in *Rolling Stone*. "Some things seem possible that wouldn't have seemed possible a few years ago, related to working with some of the guys again. Those possibilities are starting to show up again."

Henley agreed. "Glenn and I were of a like mind about several things and, now that we're older and more mature, we can apply what we've learned. If we do have another go round, I think we can do a lot of positive things. I've had ten good years of a solo career. I'm satisfied and happy. I've proven my point. And I'm happy to go back and have a little camaraderie and share some of the decisions."

Henley acknowledged at the time that "things were not quite so rosy in some quarters as they were for me", a none too veiled reference to the fact that Felder and Schmit were having a rather bumpy post-Eagles career and were very interested in getting the group back together. According to manager Azoff, quoted in a 1991 *GQ* profile of Henley, "Tim (Schmit) and Felder desperately needed this to happen and Henley felt a great loyalty to them."

The pair began writing in earnest in March 1990. On April 24-25, history of sorts was made when Frey and Schmit joined Henley and an all star line-up on stage at The Centrum in Wooster, Massachusetts, for a pair of benefit concerts to save Walden Woods. The trio ended up singing a handful of Eagles' songs. It was truly a dramatic moment and one that was not lost on Henley who, sweaty but very happy backstage after the second show, was ecstatic. "I wouldn't exactly call what you saw an Eagles reunion. But it was that band's three singers and it didn't feel like 10 years since we last sang those songs."

Henley and Frey continued to write but their plans soon ran afoul of professional considerations. "Things were going good but then my tour started and our writing thing got put back on hold. I told Glenn, 'I'll be back on June 24. I'll take 10 days off to cool out a bit and then we'll resume.'"

Frey was tightlipped about an Eagles reunion at this point, but Schmit, whose solo album 'Tell Me The Truth' came out while Henley was on tour, shortly after the Wooster benefit shows, was more than willing to put his words in Frey's mouth. "Glenn was initially real hesitant about doing this," said Schmit, "but I could see in Glenn's eyes that he was starting to dig it. Something is definitely brewing . But, as far as the entire band, I'm honestly not sure."

By the time Henley returned from his tour, Frey had apparently changed his mind. "I just wasn't ready," he confessed. "What was important to me at the time was to write songs in the morning, play golf in the afternoon and have dinner with my new beautiful wife who was pregnant with our first child. The timing was just bad for me."

Henley, in *GQ*, suspected there was more to it than timing. "The reason things fell apart was the old ghosts rearing their ugly heads. In a way those ghosts were there from the beginning. By the time The Eagles ended, Glenn and I pretty much agreed we were two different people and I guess we still were."

This was the closest to an Eagles reunion the world would get for the next three years. In fact, as late as January, the odds were climbing rather than falling. Henley was preparing songs for his next album and co-ordinating efforts on behalf of the Walden Woods preservation project. Frey, in a never ending battle to confound the critics, was getting ready to go to Nashville to record a pure country-rock album. Schmit and Walsh were also prepping solo projects while Felder, in between his quite frequent session assignments, was content to lay low with his family.

But lurking in the background, with artistic as well as monetary considerations, was Irving Azoff, constantly pushing and prodding. "Over the years everyone would ask when are you guys going to be getting back together," chuckled Felder, "and I would always say 'Well you'd better ask Irving'."

"I guess it all started with Irving," offered an amused Henley. "He's been making calls since 1980 trying to get this thing going again."

Fate, however, would ultimately take a hand in getting the band to talk. In 1993 Irving Azoff founded his own record company, Giant Records, and late in that year put out an album entitled 'Common Thread:

The Songs Of The Eagles', a compilation of Eagles' classics sung by such country stars as Clint Black and Travis Tritt. Azoff's intent was two-fold: to give the country division of his label a boost and to help raise funds for Henley's Walden Woods project.

What Azoff did not expect was that sales of the album would go through the roof. 'Common Thread' ultimately ended up selling more than three million copies and went to No. 1 on the country charts and No. 3 on the pop charts, underscoring the fact that there was still a market out there for Eagles' music and, more importantly, a reunion.

"I'm not sure we realised what a demand there was for us to get back together and play live," said a legitimately surprised Henley. "Over the years I had seen those polls you see in those showbiz magazines asking people which band you would like to see get back together and we were always at the top of the list. But I didn't think it would ever happen. But the success of the 'Common Thread' album reminded us that there was still a relatively large audience that wanted to see us get back together and tour again."

Azoff knew that the true test would be how the band would work in the Tritt video. When that experiment proved successful, Azoff, in conjunction with Frey's legal representative Peter Lopez, set the wheels in motion. The behind the scenes manoeuvring resulted in Frey and Henley having another meeting in Aspen on February 11, 1994.

"We got together in Aspen," recalled Henley. "It was just the four of us. Irving, Peter, Glenn and myself. We had lunch and we discussed it."

Azoff came away from the meeting highly optimistic. "There had been times over the years in Aspen where Glenn and Don would get together and we would try to pretend it was like old times. But it always seemed a little strained. But this time it all felt right. I could feel that things were different. That after all these years the wounds were really healed."

Lopez agreed. "It was just one of those special moments when Glenn and Don realised how much of a bond there was. They realised how much history there was between them and how much they wanted it back."

The first step in that direction was to call up Walsh and meet with him. "It seemed like the magic was still there," remembered Walsh of that meeting. "We just got together and agreed to give it a shot."

With Henley and Frey agreeing in principle to reunite The Eagles, Azoff sent out feelers to Walsh, Schmit and Felder, all of whom were only too happy to put their solo plans on hold to rejoin The Eagles.

"I got this call from Irving asking if I was interested in re-forming the band," said Felder. "Of course I was."

Following his call from Azoff, Schmit immediately rang up Henley.

"I called up Don, who over the years I had probably stayed more in touch with than the others, and said 'Hello Don? It's Timothy.' Don said 'Are you puking yet?' That was Don's way of saying are you happy about this? I told him that yes I was getting pretty excited about this. He told me 'Well hang on. It looks real good, real strong'."

But there were some reservations. "We all remember what happened the last time and we remember the good and the bad," offered Felder. "And we hope we are all older, more mature now and can learn from the mistakes."

"It was happening so fast it was getting scary," admitted Schmit. "I had to keep pinching myself to make sure it was real. I was happy about this but I was also kind of concerned."

Henley took Felder's and Schmit's concerns into account but felt the time was right to try it again. "I think one big difference is we have learned what to worry about and what not to worry about. We used to worry about and try to control everything that was going on. Now we just worry about the music."

One matter the re-forming Eagles were definitely not worried about, however, was the feelings of former members who had left before the end. "Neither Bernie or I were approached when The Eagles decided to re-form," said Meisner. "I guess their whole basic idea was this was the way the band was left and that's where they wanted to start it again. But I was feeling kind of hurt inside because the whole thing had been being planned for a year and I had not even received a telephone call about it.

By the time I found out, they had already recorded an album and were already on tour."

Meisner, who is currently working in an "Eagles-Poco kind of thing" trio with Billy Swann and Alan Rich, claimed that prior to The Eagles reuniting, he had made an attempt to bury the hatchet with the band and, in particular, Frey.

"I called Glenn up and said 'You know it might be fun to get together and talk over old times and old problems.' It was my way of saying 'Hey I'm sorry. I know I said and did a lot of things I didn't mean but inside my heart doesn't feel that way.' Glenn said 'Yeah maybe we can get together.' But he never called back."

Meisner maintained that his "feelings were hurt and so were Bernie's'. My relationship with them is real strained at this point," he admits. "And it's not even so much that they re-recorded everything so that they could keep all the artist's royalties. I guess they really hate me and that's fine with me because I've put all that stuff behind me and I can live with that.

"They're still living that fake scene, that Hollywood scene. Those guys are not living in the real world. Maybe 10 years from now they'll realise that and maybe, at that point, we can stop being mad at each other."

The feelings of Meisner and Leadon were far from the band's mind as they prepared to open their Hell Freezes Over tour May 27, 1994, at the Southern California Irvine Meadows Amphitheater. What was prominent was justifying the return and anticipating the audience's response.

"I'm prepared to be called Jurassic Rock and I'm prepared for certain people to not want to believe it is sincere and that we are just in it for the money," reflected Frey a week before the first show. "The only way we can prove ourselves is through the music. That's why we all had to be committed to this to make it work. This reunion isn't something we can just walk through. I wouldn't have gotten near this if I thought we were going to embarrass ourselves."

Embarrassing themselves musically was not a concern to Henley. "I went over to Glenn's house the other day and I had just the beginning of a song. I threw it at him and he picked up on the idea and we finished it that day. It felt wonderful to be writing with Glenn again. I left his house walking on air... just knowing that we could still do it."

Nor was Henley concerned with the idea of taking what amounted to an Eagles' greatest hits package on an extended tour. "I have a very high tolerance for repetition," he said, "which is one of the perquisites for lasting in this business. So I don't really mind going out on this tour and singing these songs over and over again. Because, as soon as you hit that first note, the audience gives you your energy. They go nuts and when you hear that roar, that's all you need to keep it going."

Friday May 27, 1994. The lights go down on the Irvine Meadows Amphitheater. Shouts and applause build. Backstage the band is waiting. Gone is the anger and animosity that marked the last time The Eagles shared a concert stage. Walsh is smiling the beatific smile, trying to come across as not being nervous but is finally betrayed by the look in his eyes. Henley's hands are moving in a subtle yet exaggerated way as he makes small talk with Schmit, Frey and Felder. Yes Felder and Frey are talking to each other; nary the hint of confrontation in the air.

"I think time really sorts out the men from the boys," philosophised Henley. "It's been a real test for us. The fact that we've been away from all this for 14 years speaks highly for the music. With this band it's not really about our image or the kind of shirts we wear or how much money we've made. It all comes down to the music. It all comes down to the work."

The announcer says "The Eagles!" The applause and shouts explode as the band hits the stage and washes over them. The band launches into the intro to 'Hotel California'. Frey picking an intricate, melancholy line, glances over at Felder at another part of the stage. They exchange a knowing smile.

The Eagles will not be fighting tonight.

Chart Singles

Take It Easy
Asylum 11005 June 24, 1972
Weeks In Top 40: 8
High Chart Position: 12

Witchy Woman
Asylum 11008 September 30, 1972
Weeks In Top 40: 10
High Chart Position: 9

Peaceful Easy Feeling
Asylum 11013 February 3, 1973
Weeks In Top 40: 6
High Chart Position: 22

Already Gone
Asylum 11036 June 22, 1974
Weeks In Top 40: 3
High Chart Position: 32

Best Of My Love
Asylum 45218 December 28, 1974
Weeks In Top 40: 14
High Chart Position: 1

One Of These Nights
Asylum 45257 June 14, 1975
Weeks In Top 40: 14
High Chart Position: 1

Lyin' Eyes
Asylum 45279 September 27, 1975
Weeks In Top 40: 11
High Chart Position: 2

Take It To The Limit
Asylum 45293 January 17, 1976
Weeks In Top 40: 14
High Chart Position: 4

New Kid In Town
Asylum 45373 December 25, 1976
Weeks In Top 40: 13
High Chart Position: 1

Hotel California
Asylum 45386 March 12, 1977
Weeks In Top 40: 15
High Chart Position: 1

Life In The Fast Lane
Asylum 45403 May 28, 1977
Weeks In Top 40: 8
High Chart Position: 11

Please Come Home For Christmas
Asylum 45555 December 23, 1978
Weeks In Top 40: 5
High Chart Position: 18

Heartache Tonight
Asylum 46545 October 13, 1979
Weeks In Top 40: 13
High Chart Position: 1

The Long Run
Asylum 46569 December 8, 1979
Weeks In Top 40: 12
High Chart Position: 8

I Can't Tell You Why
Asylum 47100 March 1, 1980
Weeks In Top 40: 12
High Chart Position: 8

Seven Bridges Road
Asylum 47100 January 1, 1981
Weeks In Top 40: 7
High Chart Position: 21

Chart Albums

EAGLES
Train Leaves Here This Morning / Tryin' / Take It Easy /
Chug All Night / Most Of Us Are Sad / Earlybird / Take The
Devil / Witchy Woman / Nightingale / Peaceful Easy Feeling
Asylum SD 5054 July 22, 1972
Weeks In Top 40: 7
High Chart Position: 22

DESPERADO
Doolin' Dalton / Twenty One / Out Of Control / Tequila
Sunrise / Desperado / Certain Kind Of Fool / Doolin' Dalton
(Instrumental) / Outlaw Man / Saturday Night / Bitter Creek /
Doolin' Dalton – Desperado (Reprise)
Asylum SD 5068 April 17, 1973
Weeks In Top 40: 0
High Chart Position: 41

ON THE BORDER
Already Gone / You Never Cry Like A Lover / Midnight
Flyer / My Man / On The Border / James Dean / Ol' 55 / Is It
True / Good Day In Hell / The Best Of My Love
Asylum 7E 1004 April 27, 1974
Weeks In Top 40: 24
High Chart Position: 17

ONE OF THESE NIGHTS
After The Thrill Is Gone / Hollywood Waltz / I Wish You
Peace / Journey Of The Sorcerer / Lyin' Eyes / One Of These
Nights / Take It To The Limit / Too Many Hands / Visions
Asylum 7E 1039 June 28, 1975
Weeks In Top 40: 43
High Chart Position: 1

EAGLES/THEIR GREATEST HITS 1971-1975
Take It Easy / Witchy Woman / Lyin' Eyes / Already Gone /
Desperado / One Of These Nights / Tequila Sunrise / Take
It To The Limit / Peaceful Easy Feeling / Best Of My Love
Asylum 6E 1052 March 6, 1976
Weeks In Top 40: 57
High Chart Position: 1

HOTEL CALIFORNIA
Hotel California / New Kid In Town / Life In The Fast
Lane / Wasted Time / Wasted Time (Reprise) / Victim Of
Love / Pretty Maids All In A Row / Try And Love Again /
The Last Resort
Asylum 6E 1084 December 25, 1976
Weeks In Top 40: 32
High Chart Position: 1

THE LONG RUN
The Long Run / I Can't Tell You Why / In The City / The
Disco Strangler / King Of Hollywood / Heartache Tonight /
Those Shoes / Teenage Jail / The Greeks Don't Want No
Freaks / The Sad Café
Asylum 5E 508 October 20, 1979
Weeks In Top 40: 36
High Chart Position: 1

EAGLES LIVE
Hotel California / Heartache Tonight / I Can't Tell You
Why / The Long Run / New Kid In Town / Life's Been Good /
Seven Bridges Road / Wasted Time / Take It To The Limit /
Doolin' Dalton (Reprise) / Desperado / Saturday Night /
All Night Long / Life In The Fast Lane / Take It Easy
Asylum BB 705 November 29, 1980
Weeks In Top 40: 16
High Chart Position: 6

EAGLES GREATEST HITS VOLUME 2
Hotel California / Heartache Tonight / Seven Bridges Road /
Victim Of Love / The Sad Café / Life In The Fast Lane / I Can't
Tell You Why / New Kid In Town / The Long Run / After The
Thrill Is Gone
Asylum 960205-1 December 1982
Weeks In Top 40: 0
High Chart Position: 52

HELL FREEZES OVER
Get Over It / Love Will Keep Us Alive / The Girl
From Yesterday / Learn To Be Still / Tequila Sunrise /
Hotel California / Wasted Time / Pretty Maids All In A Row /
I Can't Tell You Why / New York Minute / The Last Resort /
Take It Easy / In The City / Life In The Fast Lane /
Desperado
Geffen GEFC -24725 November 1994
High Chart Position: 1

Glenn Frey

Longbranch Pennywhistle
(with Longbranch Pennywhistle)
Amos AAS 7007 1969

No Fun Allowed
Asylum E1 60129 1982

The Allnighter
MCA 5501 1984

Beverly Hills Cop: Soundtrack
MCA 5547 1984

Miami Vice: Soundtrack
MCA 6150 1985

Soul Searchin'
MCA 6239 1988

Thelma And Louise: Soundtrack
MCA 10239 1991

Strange Weather
MCA 10599 1992

Glenn Frey Live
MCA 10826 1993

Solo Collection (Greatest Hits)
MCAD 11227 1995

Don Henley

Shiloh (with Shiloh)
Amos AAS7015 1970

I Can't Stand Still
Asylum E1 60048 1982

Fast Times At Ridgemont High: Soundtrack
Full Moon 60158 1982

Building The Perfect Beast
Geffen 24026 1984

Vision Quest: Soundtrack
Geffen GHS 24063 1985

The Color Of Money: Soundtrack
MCA 6189 1986

The End Of The Innocence
Geffen 24217 1989

Joe Walsh

Barnstorm
Dunhill 50130 1972

The Smoker You Drink, The Player You Get
Dunhill 50140 1973

So What
Dunhill 50171 1974

You Can't Argue With A Sick Mind
ABC 932 1976

But Seriously Folks...
Asylum 6E 141 1978

The Best Of Joe Walsh
ABC 1083 1978

FM: Soundtrack
MCA 12000 1978

The Warriors: Soundtrack
A&M SP-4761 1979

Urban Cowboy: Soundtrack
Asylum 90002 1980

There Goes The Neighborhood
Asylum 5E 523 1981

Fast Times At Ridgemont High: Soundtrack
Full Moon 60158 1982

You Bought It: You Name It
Warner 23884 1983

The Confessor
Warner 25281 1985

Got Any Gum?
Warner 25606 1987

Great Outdoors: Soundtrack
Atlantic 81859-1 1988

Ordinary Average Guy
Pyramid 47384 1991

Songs For A Dying Planet
Pyramid 48916 1992

The Beverly Hillbillies: Soundtrack
RCA 66313 1994

Robocop: A Future...Soundtrack
Rhino 71888 1995

Bernie Leadon

Bluegrass Favorites
(The Scottsville Squirrel Barkers)
Crown CST 346 1963

Of Horses, Kids And Forgotten Women
(Hearts And Flowers)
Capitol ST 2868 1968

The Fantastic Expedition (Dillard And Clark)
A&M SD-4158 1968

Through The Morning, Through The Night
(Dillard And Clark)
A&M SD-4203 1969

Burrito Deluxe (The Flying Burrito Brothers)
A&M SD-4258 1970

The Flying Burrito Brothers
(The Flying Burrito Brothers)
A&M SD-4295 1971

Natural Progressions
(The Bernie Leadon-Michael Georgiades Band)
Asylum 1107 1977

Workin' Band (The Nitty Gritty Dirt Band)
Warner 25722 1988

Randy Meisner

Randy Meisner
Asylum 6E-140 1978

FM: Soundtrack
MCA 12000 1978

One More Song
Epic 36748 1980

Randy Meisner
Epic 38121 1982

Legacy (Poco)
RCA 9694 1989

Don Felder

Flow (Flow)
CTI 1003 1970

Heavy Metal: Soundtrack
Asylum 90004 1981

Fast Times At Ridgemont High: Soundtrack
Full Moon 60158 1982

Airborne
Elektra 60295 1983

Secret Admirer: Soundtrack
MCA 5611 1985

Timothy B. Schmit

Glad (Glad)
ABC 60158 1970

Fast Times At Ridgemont High: Soundtrack
Full Moon 60158 1982

Playin' It Cool
Asylum 60359 1984

Secret Admirer: Soundtrack
MCA 5611 1985

Timothy B.
MCA 42049 1987

Tell Me The Truth
MCA 6420 1990